D0146667

The American History Series
Series Editors
John Hope Franklin, *Duke University*
Abraham S. Eisenstadt, *Brooklyn College*

Arthur S. Link
Princeton University
General Editor for History

John E. Wiltz
INDIANA UNIVERSITY

From Isolation to War, 1931-1941

Harlan Davidson, Inc.
Arlington Heights, Illinois 60004

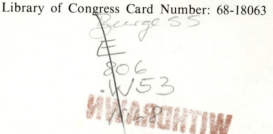

Cover illustration: Richmond *Times-Dispatch*

PRINTED IN THE UNITED STATES OF AMERICA

83   84   85EB10   9   8   7   6

EDITORS' FOREWORD

Every generation writes its own history, for the reason that it sees the past in the foreshortened perspective of its own experience. This has certainly been true of the writing of American history. The practical aim of our historiography is to offer us a more certain sense of where we are going by helping us understand the road we took in getting where we are. If the substance and nature of our historical writing is changing, it is precisely because our own generation is redefining its direction, much as the generations that preceded us redefined theirs. We are seeking a newer direction, because we are facing new problems, changing our values and premises, and shaping new institutions to meet new needs. Thus, the vitality of the present inspires the vitality of our writing about our past. Today's scholars are hard at work reconsidering every major field of our history: its politics, diplomacy, economy, society, mores, values, sexuality, and status, ethnic, and race relations. No less significantly, our scholars are using newer modes of investigation to probe the ever-expanding domain of the American past.

Our aim, in this American History Series, is to offer the reader a survey of what scholars are saying about the central themes and issues of American history. To present these themes and issues, we have invited scholars who have made notable contributions to the respective fields in which they are writing. Each volume offers the reader a sufficient factual and narrative account for perceiving the larger dimensions of its particular subject. Addressing their respective themes, our authors have undertaken, moreover, to present the conclusions derived by the principal writers on these themes. Beyond that, the authors present their own conclusions about those aspects of their respective subjects that have been matters of difference and controversy. In effect, they have written not only about where the subject stands in today's historiography but also about where they stand on their subject. Each volume closes with an extensive critical essay on the writings of the major authorities on its particular theme.

The books in this series are designed for use in both basic and advanced courses in American history. Such a series has a particular utility in times such as these, when the traditional format of our American history courses is being altered to accommodate a greater diversity of texts and reading materials. The series offers a number of distinct advantages. It extends and deepens the dimensions of course work in American history. In proceeding beyond the confines of the traditional textbook, it makes clear that the study of our past is, more than the student might otherwise infer, at once complex, sophisticated, and profound. It presents American history as a subject of continuing vitality and fresh investigation. The work of experts in their respective fields, it opens up to the student the rich findings of historical inquiry. It invites the student to join, in major fields of research, the many groups of scholars who are pondering anew the central themes and problems of our past. It challenges the student to participate actively in exploring American history and to collaborate in the creative and rigorous adventure of seeking out its wider reaches.

John Hope Franklin

Abraham S. Eisenstadt

CONTENTS

ACKNOWLEDGMENTS: I wish to express my gratitude to John Hope Franklin and Abraham S. Eisenstadt for the invitation to contribute to this series. To Douglas G. H. Hall and my colleagues at the University of the West Indies in the academic year 1965-66 I am grateful for providing such pleasant surroundings for composition of this book. The palms and poincianas swaying in the Caribbean breeze made me feel that I lived in a world removed from diplomacy and war. I want to thank Shinobu Iwamura, chairman of the Center for Southeast Asian Studies, Kyoto University, Japan, for his recollection of events and people in Japan in the 1930s. At that time Professor Iwamura was a ranking official in the Japanese government news agency. I am grateful to Justus D. Doenecke for making available unpublished materials on America's response to the Manchurian incident. My thanks also to my colleague James T. Patterson of Indiana University who criticized two chapters before going on leave to Germany. Above all, I want to thank Robert H. Ferrell who spent many hours going over this manuscript word by word, catching errors here, striking superfluous sentences and paragraphs there. Indiana colleagues and students who have submitted their prose for the "Ferrell treatment" can appreciate the value of this criticism.

ONE

In Search of Peace

It was December 8, 1941 and the first gray light of dawn was breaking over Washington. Windows of government buildings were ablaze with light, automobiles jammed the streets. At the Capitol workmen, their breath visible in the frosty morning air, were driving wooden stakes into the ground around the House of Representatives' wing. Other men followed, stringing wire cable to hold back the crowds expected later in the day. At the Capitol's main entrance barricades were going up, on which attendants tacked up signs reading "Show your passes." By mid-morning policemen, and marines with fixed bayonets, were swarming around Capitol Hill.

On this epochal Monday morning another point of activity was 1600 Pennsylvania Avenue, the White House. Crowds of curious and anxious people pressed against the iron fence, dozens of policemen patrolled the grounds. At 11:30 A.M. two open automobiles filled with Secret Service men moved into the White House driveway and rolled to a stop under the portico. Riot guns hung menacingly from the automobiles' sides. At 12:00 o'clock sharp, as six limousines drew into position, the big glass doors of the White House swung open, and into the chilly mid-day air walked President Franklin D. Roosevelt, supported by his son James, who was wearing the uniform of a marine officer. Grim-faced and silent, the President slowly descended the steps and entered a limousine bearing White House insignia. Other automobiles quickly filled with aides, officials, and members of the President's family. A moment later the cars were moving down the driveway, through the East Gate, turning right on Pennsylvania Avenue. Quiet crowds lined the streets. Skies were leaden, the temperature in the upper forties. A few brown leaves still clung to the city's larger trees.

Minutes later the presidential caravan entered the Capitol plaza and rolled to a special entrance. Onlookers broke into a cheer. His mouth tightly drawn, the President ignored the cheering, slowly lifted himself from the limousine, and went in to the office of the speaker of the House of Representatives. Members of the House were taking seats in the adjoining chamber.

Members of the Senate meanwhile were marching two-by-two from the Senate wing, down the long corridor and through the rotunda to the House side. They entered the chamber behind Majority Leader Alben W. Barkley of Kentucky and Minority Leader Charles L. McNary of Oregon. A moment later the black-robed justices of the Supreme Court, led by Harlan F. Stone, entered the chamber and marched down the center aisle. Everyone in the huge room rose in respect. The justices took seats along the edge of the well, to the left of the rostrum. At 12:24 the vice-president rapped his gavel, and again everyone stood up. Down the aisle filed the President's cabinet, led by the white-haired secretary of state, Cordell Hull. Then, at 12:29, Speaker of the House Sam Rayburn of Texas rapped for silence and announced: "The President of the United States." Automatically the members of Congress, guests at the rear of the chamber, officials, diplomats, and the handful of servicemen and ordinary citizens who had managed seats in the galleries rose to their feet. For an instant there was silence, then applause. The applause increased, but ended abruptly when Rayburn pounded his gavel. Still supported by James Roosevelt, the President appeared and slowly made his way up a ramp to the rostrum. More applause. Applause broke into cheering, and for the next two or three minutes Roosevelt received the most tumultuous ovation of his presidency. Powerful lights enveloped the President in a blazing glow, movie cameras whirred, a dozen microphones made a jagged pattern across the rostrum.

After the House chaplain offered a brief prayer the President, dressed in formal morning attire, stood alone. The large clock at his back showed 12:34, and at that moment a hush fell over the Republic as scores of millions of Americans turned to radios to receive the words of their President. Roosevelt opened a black looseleaf notebook, similar to one a child might use in school, and in restrained, staccato tones began: "Yesterday, December 7, 1941—a date which will live in infamy—the United States was suddenly and deliberately attacked by naval and air forces of the empire of Japan."

It was a drama that had played out twenty-four years before, in April 1917, when President Woodrow Wilson on an equally solemn occasion made an identical trip to the Capitol and asked Congress to declare war on Germany. Because of repetition the drama in 1941 was curiously poignant, recalling the oft-quoted remark of George Santayana that "he who does not know history is fated to repeat it."

I

When quiet finally settled over the Western Front in France in November 1918, President Wilson made plans to go to Paris for the peace conference. Over the past year and a half he had taken leadership of a crusade for democracy; now he would lead the world to a peace settlement resting on justice and supported by a League of Nations. And as the steamer *George Washington* in December 1918 slipped out of New York harbor en route to Europe the President jauntily paced the deck, smiling, full of confidence. He had support of war-weary people the world over, and when he landed in France a week later he met unparalleled enthusiasm. A Paris newspaper reported that "never has a king, never has an emperor received such a welcome."

Then something went wrong. The people of the United States rejected the peace drafted at Paris. They refused to join the League of Nations, and by 1923 Wilson's successor in the White House, Warren G. Harding, could announce that the League issue in America was "as dead as slavery." Americans were determined to keep their distance—to insulate themselves from Europe's troubles. Over the next decade and a half this "isolationist impulse," so called by the historian Selig Adler, increased, and by the mid-1930s had reached such a fervent pitch that Congress wrote isolation into law. This is not to say, however, that Americans closed their eyes entirely to the rest of the world. The historian William Appleman Williams has noted ("The Legend of Isolationism in the 1920's," *Science and Society,* Winter 1954) that Americans took considerable interest in events elsewhere in the world, and continually worked to expand their foreign trade. In Williams's view the idea of an isolated America in the 1920s "is no more than a legend." He has a point. Americans did not close their eyes and ears to the rest of the world and isolation doubtless is a poor word to describe America's position at that time. But over the decades when students of history have used the term in commenting on American diplomacy between the two world wars they have been referring to the country's unwillingness to take responsibility for keeping the peace, its determination to avoid the Old World's political difficulties; they have not suggested that the country abandoned all interest in international affairs.

What happened? What chemistry caused Americans to turn from their support of Woodrow Wilson's idealism toward the practice of what the historian Thomas A. Bailey (*The Man in the Street,* 1948) has described as "heads-in-the-sand" isolation?

The political scientist Samuel Lubell in *The Future of American Politics* (1952) has sought to explain America's interwar isolation in ethnic terms. "The two factors . . . primarily responsible for American isolation are: First, the existence of pro-German and anti-British ethnic prejudices. Second, the exploiting of these prejudices by an opposition political party." Comparing voting statistics for the 1920s and 1930s, Lubell found these prejudices widespread among Americans of German, Irish, Scandinavian, and Italian origin; the opposition party, of course, was the Republican. He writes that in the 1920s these ethnic groups for various reasons felt embittered over the outcome of the war of 1914-18. Urged on by Republicans, they reacted against the Democratic Party— Wilson's party—and all its activities, including the League of Nations and an "international" approach to world affairs. As a new war threatened in the 1930s these same groups—Germans, Irish, Italians—saw that another involvement in Europe's controversies would find the United States once more on the side of Great Britain, against Germany and Italy. To them such a prospect was anathema. Since there was no chance of an American alliance with Germany and Italy, the only alternative to standing with Britain was isolation.

The ideas of Lubell have sparked interest among historians, and in 1965 were the subject of a session at the annual meeting of the Organization of American Historians at Kansas City. But most historians have found it incredible that the ethnic groups cited by Lubell, comprising a small minority of the national population, could move the country to isolation. Historians, moreover, examining a range of source materials, have noted other factors that contributed to the isolationist mood of the 1920s and 1930s. In the words of Manfred Jonas (*Isolationism in America,* 1966), "an examination of isolationist policies and the statements of the movement's leading spokesmen confirms that isolationism during the period just before the Second World War was not essentially an ethnic matter."

Jonas has noted that isolation was an old habit, rooted in American tradition. The habit had its origins in several sources. One was geography. From its birth the United States had enjoyed security to a degree unparalleled in the history of modern nations. The Atlantic and later the Pacific served as giant barriers against aggression from Europe or Asia, and this country's neighbors in the Western Hemisphere were too weak to threaten an attack. Another source was economics. The North American continent, awaiting axe and plow, offered such rewards that Americans inevitably turned their energy to exploration of their own empire. Then there were politics and patriotism. Like Thomas Jefferson, most Americans saw the Old World as corrupt, quarrelsome, autocratic—the antithesis of democratic America. Americans wanted their country to be as little like Europe as possible. They remembered the counsel of their first President, George Washington, who in his famous Farewell Address of September 1796 warned of "the insidious wiles of foreign influence," urged "as little political connection as possible" with foreign countries, noted the advantages of "our detached and distant situation." Down to the closing years of the nineteenth century no responsible politician dared challenge Washington's logic, and isolation became identified with Americanism. In an essay in the volume *Isolation and Security* (1957), Alexander DeConde has written that isolation became "a sacred legacy on the same lofty level as religion."

At the end of the nineteenth century the isolationist tradition seemed to weaken. Under Presidents William McKinley and Theodore Roosevelt the United States acquired an overseas empire and began to exert influence in many parts of the world. President Wilson sent American youths to France in 1917-18, and when the war ended sought to take the United States into the League of Nations. According to Selig Adler (*The Isolationist Impulse,* 1957), however, the departure from old lines of thought had been more apparent than real. Hence it was easy for the isolationist habit to reassert itself in the 1920s, and in 1935 Representative Maury Maverick (D) of Texas was expressing a popular sentiment when he announced: "In our Revolution against the British, Lafayette came over here, and Baron von Steuben, also a foreigner, came to train our Revolutionary troops, and we were glad to have them; but we do not like foreigners any more."

II

DeConde, Jonas, and other students of isolation have emphasized that disillusion over the results of the conflict of 1914-18 turned Americans inward. Selig Adler (*The Uncertain Giant,* 1965) has described the "giant recoil" against the "over there" spirit of 1917-18, and William E. Leuchtenburg (*The Perils of Prosperity,* 1958) writes that in the 1920s the Great War—as people continued to call it—became "a dirty, unheroic war which few men remembered with any emotion save distaste."

Why had this happened?

America's leaders, historians agree, had oversold the World War. Instead of presenting American participation as a matter of national interest, distasteful but necessary, they made it a crusade for democracy. At the peace conference and after, however, there seemed to be as much selfish nationalism in the world as before, and if anything less democracy. Americans felt disgusted for having been so foolish as to become party to Europe's war. Despite Wilson's exalted ideas the war had been a European affair, fought over European problems, for European ends. No American interest, the public concluded, had been at stake. Millions of people agreed with Senator Homer T. Bone (D) of Washington when he declared in 1935 that "the Great War . . . was utter social insanity, and was a crazy war, and we had no business in it at all."

Other Americans were disillusioned by the vindictive peace the victors had imposed at Paris in 1919. These were people who had thrilled to President Wilson's idea of a "peace without victory" and hailed his Fourteen Points, including Point 14 urging a League of Nations. When they learned that in Paris's superheated atmosphere Wilson had compromised principle and acquiesced in a conqueror's peace, they rejected the League and decided that the United States must live in isolation. As editors of the liberal periodical *New Republic* put it in 1919, Americans had hoped that "they would participate in a Europe so chastened by the war that the interests of a lasting peace would take precedence over every other national advantage. The European governments have chosen differently. Well and good. That must be their affair. It certainly should not be America's affair in the sense that American lives and American interests are entangled in it."

In his book on isolation in the latter 1930s Manfred Jonas has pointed out that revised ideas as to how the United States had become involved in the World War heightened America's postwar disillusion. One idea was that Americans had become aroused against Germany because of mistaken notions about the causes of the war in Europe. From the outset of hostilities in summer 1914 most Americans accepted the view that the Germans were the aggressors. Germans fired the first shots on the Western Front, raped Belgium, plunged into France. When America entered the war in 1917 leaders in Washington assured the people that Germany had started the war because of militarism and sheer will to power. But after the war some writers concluded that Germany had not been exclusively responsible. The historian Sidney Bradshaw Fay countered the idea of German culpability in a series of articles in the *American Historical Review,* and in his book *The Origins of the World War* (1928) wrote that "Germany did not plot a European War, did not want one, and made genuine, though too belated efforts to avert one." Another historian, Albert Jay Nock, brought out a pamphlet entitled "The Myth of a Guilty Nation" (1922) which absolved Germany and deplored American support of the Allies. And the sociologist-historian Harry Elmer Barnes assigned responsibility for the war "in about this order: Austria, Russia, Serbia, France, Germany, and England." Why had Americans failed to grasp the "truth" about the war? Many people, including C. Hartley Grattan (*Why We Fought,* 1929) and Walter Millis (*Road to War,* 1935), found an answer in Allied propaganda, a view that was reinforced when some British officials admitted that during the war the Allies had played on American opinion by lies and deception.

Then, as Jonas and many others have noted, some people had the idea that American entry in the World War had been the work of unscrupulous Wall Street bankers. It was common knowledge that American financiers had arranged huge loans to the Allied governments. When it appeared that the Allies might not win, the bankers—so the argument went—feared for their money and pressed leaders in Washington to take the country to war. If proponents of this "devil theory" offered no proof, the notion of Wall Street responsibility for American involvement in Europe's bloodbath nonetheless made sense to millions of Americans, strengthened the view that entry in the war in 1917 had been a mistake, and heightened the national determination to stay clear of any new European conflict.

Another source of American disillusion in the postwar era, and also a source of disenchantment toward Europe, was the controversy over the war debts. While opposing armies struggled late in 1914 less than sixty miles from Paris, the Allies looked across the Atlantic to the United States for financial support, and, as mentioned, working through such banking houses as J. P. Morgan & Company, borrowed enormous sums. When the United States joined the war in 1917 the government opened its checkbook to the Allies. After the war the Allies managed to pay interest to the financiers and bondholders but appealed for cancellation of debts owed the United States government—*i.e.* the American people. Such talk irked Americans, who calculated that the war had been a European venture, that Europe had been the beneficiary. They felt that Europeans should be grateful for American intervention and pay their debts to the last penny. Most Americans agreed with President Calvin Coolidge, who allegedly said: "They hired the money, didn't they?" Europeans, of course, saw matters differently. Believing defeat of Germany in America's as well as Europe's interest, they figured that from 1914 to 1917 they had fought America's fight. They also noted that the war, while crushing the economies of Europe, had brought prosperity to America, and in Europe the initials "U.S." now stood for "Uncle Shylock" who was demanding his pound of flesh from people who had shed blood in the common cause while America took profits. Europe's views about the debts had scant effect, and Americans continued to insist that the Allies honor their obligations. When the Allies remained in default Americans became increasingly convinced of the corruption of Europe, and according to Manfred Jonas the war debt problem was one argument for isolation into the late 1930s.

Climaxing disillusion over the war was the Great Depression of the 1930s, ushered in by the stock market collapse of autumn 1929. Some economists and many non-economists thought that the war had planted the seeds of the Depression a decade before. They reasoned that deflation must follow inflation; bust follows boom. During the war Americans had enjoyed unprecedented prosperity, and in 1929 the time had come to pay for the good living. Looking into the future, proponents of such ideas saw a repetition of the pattern if the United States became involved in a new war. There would be a boom. Bust inevitably follows boom. *Ergo,* to avoid another bust avoid war.

Adler in *The Isolationist Impulse* has observed that new attitudes about war helped turn Americans to isolation. War had lost its glamor. Reflecting on war, people in the years after 1918 were not inclined to envision cavalry charges with banners flying and sabers flashing. They saw mud, barbed wire, fear, desolation, death. Reinforcing the new image of war were such books as Erich Maria Remarque's *All Quiet on the Western Front*. Shocked by the horror of modern war, many Americans in the two decades after the armistice of 1918 developed scrupulous consciences about war. Some concluded that most wars in history had been morally wrong. Others wrestled with the morality of killing enemies even in a "just" war. As a young man crudely expressed it in a letter to Senator Gerald P. Nye (R) of North Dakota in 1934: "As a potential soldier, I object to the prospect of becoming cannon fodder in the 'next war'; as a future taxpayer, I object to enriching arms manufacturers by impoverishing my fellow Americans; and, most important, as a Christian, I object to preparing to run a bayonet through my brother from another country."

There was also the legacy of the recent war, including the post-1918 demand for veterans' bonuses. Privates risking their lives in France had received $1.25 a day, while friends in the factories and shipyards at home had earned ten times as much. There was logic in the argument that the country owed veterans some "adjusted compensation." Logic did not make attractive the idea of taxes for payment of bonuses. And where would the bonus business end? Historians could remind the country that the amount of money paid to Civil War veterans over the years after Appomattox had exceeded the cost of the conflict in 1861-65. There were of course the permanent victims of the 1917-18 war, men who had suffered from shrapnel and gas in the crusade for democracy. The country had to care for them. That took money, and these sad men were living reminders of the reality of war.

Such writers as Manfred Jonas and Wayne S. Cole (*America First,* 1953) have thought the politics of domestic reform provided another incentive for isolation between the wars, particularly in the late 1930s. During the years 1901-17, the so-called Progressive era, reformers in America had moved from triumph to triumph, reaching a climax in the New Freedom program of President Wilson. As the United States drew closer to war in 1915-17, most liberals urged that the nation keep out of Europe's conflict lest involvement stifle domestic reform legislation. When the country entered the war in 1917 their fears came true; the reform program ended, and leaders of business returned to seats of power in government. The worst was yet to come, for war brought a conservative reaction in American politics. Laboring in a political wilderness, progressives in the postwar decade felt even greater hostility toward war, seeing it as an enemy of reform, a harbinger of reaction. Then came the New Deal, and a renaissance of the progressive movement. Recalling the experience of two decades before, some progressives, according to Jonas and Cole, feared that a new intervention in war might bring nullification of the liberal gains since 1933. On the other hand, political conservatives supported isolation out of fear that involvement in war might bring further weakening of the capitalist system.

III

Urging on the quest for peace in the years between the world wars was an array of peace organizations. This so-called peace movement has attracted the attention of historians, but to date there has been no satisfactory study of its organization and tactics, successes and failures. The best summary is an essay by Robert H. Ferrell, "The Peace Movement," in Alexander DeConde (editor), *Isolation and Security*.

Though not responsible for creating the conditions that aroused Americans for peace, the peace societies labored mightily to prevent any weakening of the national resolve to avoid war. They also campaigned for programs and policies they thought would advance peace. Some were religious groups which saw war as the great evil of the time; most had the sole purpose of crusading for peace. Among the latter organizations were the League of Nations Association, Woodrow Wilson Foundation, American Committee for the Cause and Cure of War, National Council for Prevention of War, Women's International League for Peace and Freedom, American Committee for the Outlawry of War, and an organization known by the initials "S.O.S."—Stop Organized Slaughter.

The peace movement in the United States originated in the

early years of the nineteenth century, after the Napoleonic wars in Europe. First was the Massachusetts Peace Society, organized in 1815. The American Peace Society, most influential of the early groups, appeared in 1828. The movement in truth did not amount to much in its infancy, for no enemies threatened the United States and far more pressing concerns for humanitarians were problems of Negro slavery, care of the insane, inhuman prison conditions. The Mexican War of 1846-48 and the Civil War of 1861-65 proved the futility of the peace movement, and after Appomattox, when Americans turned to industrialization and westward expansion, the movement nearly expired. Even Andrew Carnegie's dramatic gift of ten million dollars in 1910 for establishment of the Carnegie Endowment for International Peace failed to strike much fire in America. Then, after the First World War, the peace movement came alive, and in the two decades that followed, until the attack on Pearl Harbor, it reached a pinnacle of influence. Following the Second World War the movement went into eclipse, its remnants clustering along the East River in New York where they served as adjuncts of the American delegation to the United Nations.

Between the wars the peace movement had two "wings," which one might label as conservative and radical. Believing that peace required international co-operation, the conservative wing— the Carnegie Endowment, World Peace Foundation, Woodrow Wilson Foundation, League of Nations Association—did not push the country toward isolation. More important were the radical groups—the Women's International League, National Council for Prevention of War, Committee on Militarism in Education, Peace Heroes Memorial Society, War Resisters' League, American Committee for the Outlawry of War, American Committee for the Cause and Cure of War. Like the conservatives, radicals at first favored international co-operation, only to swing sharply toward isolation in the 1930s when the League of Nations proved unable to organize collective efforts to counter aggression. Other marks of radical organizations were a rampant anti-militarism and an impatience to rid the world of the "war habit." In the radical view time was short, for at any moment the "militarists" might seize the initiative and plunge the world into war. Robert Ferrell has written that this sense of urgency gave radical pacifists a zeal unmatched in conservative circles. Radical groups, one should add, were in no sense mass organizations; membership was small, funds limited. At its peak the radical movement had fewer than a hundred full-time workers in Washington and New York; but because of skillful organization, national disillusion over the World War, and their own frenetic energy, these people had a profound influence on American opinion.

Occasionally a comic note crept into the peace movement, such as with the antics of the Veterans of Future Wars, a college peace organization invented by eight Princeton undergraduates in 1936. The historian Ronald Schaffer ("The Veterans of Future Wars," *Yes,* January 1962) has described how the Veterans demanded an immediate bonus of $1,000 for every man between ages eighteen and thirty-six, arguing that many men in that age-group would not survive the "next war" and therefore deserved bonuses before going into battle. The Veterans paraded with overseas caps worn at right angles to the usual position, and members greeted one another with a fascist-like salute, right arm extended but with palm upturned as though seeking a handout. For college women the Veterans set up a Future Gold Star Mothers auxiliary and demanded that the government award the women pensions for trips to Europe so they could visit grave sites of their future sons and husbands. In a parade near the Columbia University campus a drum major twirled a crutch, leading 150 girls dressed as nurses or war widows who carried "war orphan" dolls, and were followed by 200 young men displaying signs like "You too can learn to play a machine gun."

Apart from railing against war and teaching "peace habits," what were the objects of the peace movement between the wars?

Ferrell has written that disarmament was a cause dear to pacifists, conservative and radical; and both groups supported the disarmament conferences of the 1920s and early 1930s. In their view bulging arsenals were, like tinderboxes, ignited by the slightest spark—such as the assassination of a European archduke. Recalling Europe's armament stocks in the years before 1914, pacifists agreed with Britain's wartime foreign minister Sir Edward Grey that "the enormous growth of armaments in Europe . . . made war inevitable."

Another pacifist enthusiasm was "outlawry of war." Put forth early in the 1920s, the idea of outlawing war did not catch on until 1927, when Charles A. Lindbergh's solo flight over the Atlantic from New York to Paris brought an outpouring of Franco-American friendship. To capitalize on these sentiments the French foreign minister Aristide Briand engaged in what Ferrell in *Peace in Their Time* (1952) has called "airplane diplomacy," proposing a pact between the United States and France that would bind the two countries never to go to war against each other. One of Europe's most clever diplomats, Briand enlisted the help of the American peace movement, and pacifists began to press President Coolidge to sign with France. The State Department suspected that Briand was seeking virtual alliance with the United States to guarantee France against possible resurgence of German power, and made a counterproposal. If a bilateral treaty was a good idea, why not a multilateral treaty pledging all nations to renounce war? Known as a man of peace—he was a former winner of the Nobel Peace Prize—Briand hardly could refuse the American suggestion. As for the peace movement, it considered the American proposal a splendid idea, and waged a tremendous campaign for a multilateral agreement outlawing war that resulted in the Kellogg-Briand Pact of 1928. Pacifists hailed the treaty as the greatest step toward peace in human history. More cynical people called it "solemn ballyhoo" and an "international kiss."

Then there were the munitions makers. Long considered a menace to peace, arms manufacturers entered the spotlight when the Women's International League in 1932 urged the United States Senate to investigate the trade in munitions. The W.I.L. received support from other pacifist groups, and early in 1934 Senator Nye agreed to sponsor a resolution for an arms inquiry. While the resolution was pending, the periodical *Fortune* published a sensational article entitled "Arms and Men" purporting to prove that arms makers were a major cause of war. At the same time two books appeared, *Iron, Blood and Profits* by George Seldes, and *Merchants of Death* by Helmuth C. Engelbrecht and Frank C.

Hanighen. According to the latter authors, "the arms maker has risen and grown powerful, until today he is one of the most dangerous factors in world affairs—a hindrance to peace, a promoter of war." Such ideas reached a national audience when *Merchants of Death* became a Book-of-the-Month Club selection and "Arms and Men" appeared in a condensed version in *Reader's Digest*.

The Senate adopted Nye's resolution, and over the next two years a special committee, popularly known as the Nye Committee, held up the arms trade to public scrutiny. It exhibited some interesting documents, such as one by an agent of the Remington Arms Company in 1933: "The Paraguay and Bolivia fracas appears to be coming to a termination, so business from that end is probably finished. We certainly are in one hell of a business, where a fellow has to wish for trouble so as to make a living, the only consolation being, however, that if we don't get the business someone else will. It would be a terrible state of affairs if my conscience started to bother me now." This document inspired Engelbrecht to another book, *One Hell of a Business*. But in truth the Nye Committee failed to prove munitions makers an important cause of war.

The Nye Committee also studied the idea that Wall Street had "dragged" the United States into the World War in 1917. Again it found little evidence, and when in February 1936 it completed the investigation of J. P. Morgan & Company, Nye conceded that he and his colleagues had proved nothing to the detriment of Morgan and his house.

Still, at the same time the Nye Committee was failing to prove its pet ideas, the peace movement reached a peak of influence and announced its solution for keeping America out of war: total isolation. Ignoring the troubles of the rest of the world was not enough; the United States should complete its insulation by cutting economic ties with warring nations as well. This idea attracted wide support and, as Chapter Three shows, resulted in a series of congressional acts.

As the world fell toward war in the late 1930s the peace movement remained as vocal as ever, and in 1938 secured approval of many congressmen for a constitutional amendment sponsored by Representative Louis Ludlow of Indiana providing that, except in event of an invasion of the United States or its territories, the authority of Congress to declare war should not become effective until confirmed by a majority vote in a national referendum. In Ludlow's words, "my war-referendum peace resolution . . . is intended to prevent our precious boys—the flower of American manhood—from being drawn into another world war which appears at the moment to be looming over the world horizon." Fortunately a majority in Congress agreed with Senator Arthur H. Vandenberg (R) of Michigan that "it would be as sensible to require a town meeting before permitting the fire department to put out the blaze."

The attention given the Ludlow Amendment was misleading, for, as Robert S. Divine has intimated in *The Illusion of Neutrality* (1962), pacifist influence by 1938 was beginning to wane as the problem of war and peace slipped from abstraction to reality. It was clear to most Americans by then that international affairs were more complicated than the peace movement had led them to believe. As Manfred Jonas has written, the pacifists had moreover become aware of a range of dilemmas. Could the United States remain faithful to its heritage as a beacon of democracy and at the same time stand by while democracy perished in Europe? Was it true that a general war in Europe or Asia need not touch the interests of the United States? After the outbreak of war in Europe in September 1939 the several dilemmas became more acute, and Wayne Cole has described how radical pacifists became entangled with the "America First" movement, which preferred an Axis victory to American involvement. Conservative peace groups wanted to support the British. Debate became increasingly sharp, then ended abruptly—on December 7, 1941.

So it was, in the decades between the two world wars, that Americans determined to isolate themselves from "foreign" embroilments. Reinforced from many sources, this isolationist urge derived essentially from a longing for peace. The 1917-18 crusade for democracy seemed to have turned into a crusade against war. Carried on in the name of humanitarianism, Christianity, and Americanism, the new crusade "caught on," and peace became an obsession for millions of Americans. The word "peace" took on a theological quality; it struck a chord whenever it found its way into a sermon, speech, or prayer. And when President Harding voiced moving sentiments about peace he was not indulging in "bloviation," as he was wont to call some of his lesser oratory; Harding and others meant what they said about peace.

Through the decade of the 1920s the isolationist impulse manifested itself in hostility to the League of Nations and refusal to accept responsibility for peace. Otherwise Americans were willing to participate in disarmament conferences, discuss ways to strengthen international law, or enter a treaty to outlaw war. Then came the 1930s and collapse of the Paris settlement of 1919. Fearing another general war, Americans added a new dimension to their isolationism: if war enveloped other parts of the world the flames must not scorch America. Let the rest of the world destroy itself; America must live. The historian Charles A. Beard captured this sentiment in 1935 when he wrote: "We tried once to right European wrongs, to make the world safe for democracy. Even in the rosiest view the experiment was not a great success. . . . [Isolation] may be no better, for aught anyone actually knows. But we nearly burnt our house down with one experiment; so it seems not wholly irrational to try another line." In view of the international uncertainties of the 1930s the Beardian logic was difficult to confute.

TWO

Manchuria

When New Yorkers scanned the front page of the *Times* on the morning of September 19, 1931 their eyes moved uneasily to the lead story describing a compromise between Governor Franklin D. Roosevelt and the Republican majority in the Albany legislature on the issue of unemployment relief. For this was the age of the Great Depression, and problems of economic crisis commanded attention. Turning to the opposite side of the page, they saw a two-column headline that Japanese troops had seized the Manchurian city of Mukden. The accompanying story reported that three companies of Chinese soldiers on the night of September 18 (Tokyo time) had begun destroying tracks of the Japanese-owned South Manchuria Railway at a village three miles from Mukden. According to dispatches datelined Tokyo, Japanese troops had driven off the Chinese, but the Chinese counterattacked with machine guns and cannon. Special trains reportedly were speeding fresh Japanese battalions to the scene of hostilities, and Japanese air squadrons based in Korea were preparing to strike in Manchuria.

In a subsequent clarification Japanese officials claimed that a small explosive charge planted by Chinese soldiers had ripped away twenty-one inches of South Manchuria track. Nobody saw the gap, and there was no proof in the collection of bent spikes and splintered crossties which the Japanese exhibited a few days later to foreign newsmen. The Japanese, moreover, found it difficult to explain how the Mukden Express had passed over the line a few minutes after the alleged explosion. (They said the train had jumped the gap.)

As the Tokyo War Crimes Trial in 1946 established, the Mukden incident was a fraud, manufactured by Japanese army officers without consent of civil authorities in Tokyo. But in September 1931 the Japanese accused the Chinese, moved troops across the frontier from Korea, and in a few months, claiming they were pursuing Chinese bandits, occupied most of Manchuria.

Readers of *The New York Times* and other newspapers in September 1931 did not comprehend what had happened; but the peace put together at Paris in 1919 and buttressed by the Treaties of Washington (1921-22) and the Kellogg-Briand Pact (1928) had suffered its first serious fracture. The world was on the way to the Second World War.

I

If the Manchurian incident of 1931 was a beginning, it also was part of a stream of events that had begun in the 1850s, when Commodore Matthew C. Perry, under orders of President Millard Fillmore, moved into Yedo (Tokyo) Bay with four smoke-belching warships and persuaded the Japanese to accept a commercial treaty with the United States. Thus ended more than two centuries of Japanese isolation from the rest of the world. Through the door cracked open by Perry flowed the ideas of Europe and America. The result was a veritable revolution of Japanese society, for as Edwin O. Reischauer has written (*The United States and Japan*, 1957), "new wines cannot be poured into old bottles, and Western trade and diplomatic and military techniques were decidedly new wines for the old and decaying bottles of Tokugawa feudalism." Factories went up across the Japanese islands, a modern army and navy appeared, the people began to look outward. Renewal of an old rivalry with China over Korea led to a war in 1894-95 which Japan won easily, and at the peace table the Japanese extracted concessions in Manchuria. Then came frustration. Russia, France, and Germany objected to new arrangements in Manchuria and compelled the Japanese to surrender their conquest.

When in the next few years the Russians cynically elbowed their way into the Manchurian territory they had insisted Japan relinquish in 1895, and also began casting glances toward Korea —"the arrow pointed at the heart of Japan"—the Japanese prepared to act. They made an alliance with Great Britain (1902), and in 1904 launched a successful attack against Russian forces in the Far East. By the Treaty of Portsmouth (1905), engineered by the American President Theodore Roosevelt, Japan received important Russian holdings in Manchuria, including the naval base of Port Arthur and beginnings of a line that became the South Manchuria Railway. Subsequent agreements with China ratified Japan's new position in Manchuria, and to protect their interests in the "leasehold" the Japanese were empowered to station troops in a narrow "railway zone."

How did the United States respond to the "new Japan"?

Reischauer has written that in the latter decades of the nineteenth century Americans felt enthusiasm for Japan, "a picture-postcard land of beauty and quaintness." They took satisfaction in little Japan's victory over China and a decade later applauded the triumph over Russia. Reischauer believes that President Roosevelt's affection for Japan inspired his leadership in securing the Treaty of Portsmouth—"before the shaky Japanese economy gave way and robbed Japan of the fruits of her military victories over the Russians in Manchuria."

Still, the United States had commercial interests in China and with acquisition of the Philippines in 1898 became a Far Eastern power. The government in Washington necessarily viewed Japan's new strength with misgiving. Fearing for its trade with China, the United States in 1899-1900 persuaded Japan, and also the powers of Europe, to accept an "open door" in China—*i.e.* to exercise no commercial discrimination in the "spheres of interest" they were staking out in China and preserve China's independence and territorial integrity. At the same time, as Japan moved beyond its own islands, the United States worried over the Philippines, and in agreements in 1905 (the so-called Taft-Katsura memorandum) and 1908 (Root-Takahira agreement) the Americans recognized Japan's position in Korea and Manchuria in return for Japanese guarantees that they would keep hands off in the Philippines.

Japan in 1910 annexed Korea. Then, while Europe was convulsed in the World War, the Tokyo government in January 1915, seeking to enlarge Japanese holdings in Manchuria and weaken the Chinese government, placed "twenty-one demands" before China. Over American protests the Japanese in May secured most of the demands in a treaty with China. Fearing that Japan might ally herself with Germany, the United States moderated its position in Far Eastern affairs when it entered the European war in spring 1917. The result was the Lansing-Ishii agreement (November 1917) recognizing Japan's "special interests" in China.

The end of the World War brought no weakening of Japanese ambition. At the Paris Peace Conference the Japanese overcame the opposition of the American President, Woodrow Wilson, and secured Germany's economic holdings in China's Shantung Peninsula. Via a League of Nations mandate they also gained Germany's islands in the Pacific north of the equator. When in 1919 the European Allies and the United States decided to terminate the intervention in Siberia—begun in 1918 to prevent supplies previously sent to Russia from falling into Bolshevik, and perhaps German hands—the Japanese declined to withdraw. Hoping to bring to power in Siberia by intrigue a pro-Japanese regime that one day might deliver the territory to themselves, the Japanese saw their military contingent as an instrument for achieving that end. In 1920-21 the United States and Japan quarreled over the island of Yap, a cable station in the Carolines, between Guam and the Philippines.

If Americans found amusement in the jingle "Yap for the Yappers," the government in Washington took a more serious view of Japanese maneuvers in the western Pacific and East Asia. Adding to the concern of America's leaders was the Anglo-Japanese alliance of 1902. Since the War of 1812 American security had depended in no small measure on the British navy. They now had to ponder the consequences of drifting into war with Japan and finding the British navy on the side of the enemy.

War with Japan? It did seem a possibility in the years after the World War, especially if one took seriously the fulminations of Japanese military leaders. From the Russo-Japanese War—which Reischauer calls "the high-water mark of Japanese-American friendship"—relations between the United States and Japan had deteriorated. The deterioration had begun when the Treaty of Portsmouth contained no provision for a Russian indemnity. Although the military situation at the time of the peace conference gave the Japanese no leverage to compel an indemnity, the people of Japan blamed Theodore Roosevelt, and the result was a wave of anti-Americanism across the Japanese islands. Next came the insolent order by the San Francisco board of education in 1906 directing Japanese-American schoolchildren to attend segregated Oriental schools. The anti-American impulse in Japan increased. Finally, the United States had proved the main obstacle to Japanese expansion during the World War and later.

Beginning around 1919, therefore, many Japanese, especially military men, talked wildly about war with the United States. General Kojiro Sato in his book *If Japan and America Fight* (1921) expressed the sentiments of many of his compatriots when he accused the United States of hypocritically demanding that others observe the "open door" in China while harboring imperialist ambitions of its own. As for war, Sato recognized America's industrial power but felt confident that the "indomitable will" of the Japanese people would assure their ultimate triumph.[1]

How much credence leaders in Washington gave to the bellicose words of Japanese militants at that time is hard to assess, but a major object of American diplomacy at the Washington Conference of 1921-22—best remembered for its naval disarmament agreement—was to deal with problems of Japanese expansion. From Washington there emerged the Four-Power Treaty (the

---

[1] Sato's views appear in Robert J. C. Butow, *Tojo and the Coming of the War* (1961).

United States, Japan, Britain, and France) ending the Anglo-Japanese alliance and pledging the signatories to respect each other's holdings in the Pacific. The Nine-Power Treaty (the same four, plus Belgium, China, Italy, Portugal, and the Netherlands) committed signatories to America's "open door" policy in China. In the Five-Power Treaty (United States, Britain, Japan, France, and Italy) the United States and Britain paid for abrogating the 1902 alliance and Japan's pledge of good behavior: they accepted tonnage ratios in "capital" ships that guaranteed Japanese naval supremacy in the western Pacific and agreed to erect no new fortifications or naval bases in that area.

The treaties of Washington brought an improvement in Jappanese-American relations. There was a setback in 1924, when Congress insulted the Japanese by writing into the new immigration law a provision excluding immigrants from Japan. Still, moderates had taken power in Tokyo, the influence of the army was in decline, and the Japanese seemed to have put aside those dreams of expansion which in the previous decade had produced friction with the United States.

Meanwhile there was ferment in China. After tottering for many years the ancient Manchu dynasty had collapsed in 1911-12. There followed a long period of social and political turmoil, but in the 1920s a national leader appeared, General Chiang Kai-shek. Under Chiang the Chinese achieved with breathtaking speed a measure of unity and a national consciousness hitherto unknown in that land which Western observers had long considered "the sleeping giant" of East Asia. Driven by patriotism and the dream of a better life for his country's hundreds of millions of people, Chiang determined to pursue a strong foreign policy aimed at eliminating foreigners' privileges. A major target was Japanese holdings in southern Manchuria, and indeed Robert J. C. Butow (*Tojo and the Coming of the War*) has written that "whereas the British had previously been the chief object of the antiforeignism stimulated by China's new nationalistic fervor, the Japanese now suddenly became the focus of Chinese hatred."

To counter the Japanese, Chiang's government persuaded several million Chinese to migrate to what Butow calls "the tremendously rich treasure house" of Manchuria. Immigrants would emphasize Chinese ownership of the province (the connection between Manchuria and China proper always had been tenuous) and encourage economic development. The government also urged the boycotting of goods bearing the label "made in Japan."

But China's leaders saw that the key to Japan's position in Manchuria was the South Manchuria Railway. To get rid of the Japanese, then, China had only to ruin the Japanese-owned railroad. Circumvention of the South Manchuria with parallel roads should accomplish that, and late in the 1920s Chiang's government encouraged the local warlord to link one Chinese line with another, and put down a section of main track here and a spur there.

Robert H. Ferrell has written in *Kellogg; Stimson* (Volume XI in *The American Secretaries of State and Their Diplomacy*) that "the Chinese should never have tried such a transparent bit of maneuvering," for "the South Manchuria was a thread on which Japan had strung huge economic holdings." Manchuria's lumber, coal, iron, soybeans, and steel fed the Japanese economy, and those economic advantages became more important in 1930 when the Great Depression struck Japan. In one year the export of raw silk plunged by half, and by summer 1931 Japan's economic situation was desperate. Compounding the problem was its continued population growth. By 1931 sixty-five million Japanese were squeezed into an area smaller than the American state of Texas.

Other twists of history compounded the risk of tampering with Japan's position in Manchuria. The blood of Japanese soldiers had fallen on Manchuria's soil, making the leasehold a sort of hallowed ground. Then Japan's ancient rival Russia had been stirring recently in northern Manchuria. Reminiscent of the Russo-Japanese battles of 1904-05, and also threatening communism in East Asia, Russia's moves aroused Japanese patriots and stiffened their resolve to brook no nonsense from China.

Protecting the leasehold was one thing, but in the 1920s some Japanese had begun to have even larger dreams. Why should Japan merely hang on in Manchuria? The Chinese never had done much with the territory. Despite the recent Chinese migration, it was essentially a frontier area of untapped mineral wealth. By expanding from the railway zone the Japanese could broaden their industrial base, resolve food problems, and establish settlements to absorb surplus population. General Sato in *If Japan and America Fight* had declared that "a tree must have its roots." Britain had roots, stretching to Africa, India, Australia, and Canada. The roots of the United States, he wrote, reached into Central and South America. Japan too must have roots—unless it were to shrivel and die.

The more Japan's patriots pondered—especially after onset of the economic crisis—the more alluring the possibilities became. Manchuria would guard the home islands and Korea against the despicable Russians and their communist ideas, and become a link between Japan and China, bringing those countries into a giant economic bloc that would end Occidental exploitation and thwart Russian communism. This bloc would become a magnet, attracting all peoples of East Asia. Who would lead this "new order"? As Paul W. Schroeder (*The Axis Alliance and Japanese-American Relations, 1941,* 1958) has written, it would be the country having a superior culture, advanced technology, and a unified population. Namely, Japan.

Distressed by the country's problems and incensed by Chinese maneuvers, the civil government in Tokyo nonetheless was seeking peaceful solutions and entertained no grand design for a new adventure in imperialism. The government was fairly liberal (and indeed seemed to be evolving into a Western-style democracy). Still, civil authorities labored under serious difficulties. Factionalism and corruption ravaged Japan's political parties. The feudal tradition, a strong force in Japanese society, subverted democratic ideas and, as Richard Storry demonstrates in *The Double Patriots* (1957), boiling just beneath the surface of life was a fanatical nationalism.

A focus of this superheated nationalism was the army. The army's prestige in the country was at a low ebb, and the officers, piqued by cuts in military appropriations, shabby equipment, and short rations, were contemptuous of the government. They accused the government of corruption and incompetence, of being "soft on China," of resorting to endless negotiations while the Chinese besmirched Japan's honor.

Sadako N. Ogata in his narrative study *Defiance in Manchuria* (1964) has written that by late summer 1931 the young officers determined the time had come to act. A world disarmament conference was in the offing (it convened at Geneva the following

spring), and remembering how civil leaders had acquiesced in re-
duction of Japan's naval power at London the previous year, military officers feared emasculation of the army. As the historian
Armin Rappaport has written (*Henry L. Stimson and Japan,
1931-33*, 1963), a dramatic stroke at the present moment would
restore the army's prestige, prove the need of a strong military
establishment, and undermine domestic advocates of disarmament.
Inevitably thoughts turned to Manchuria, where a bold action also
would open the way for a new and glorious imperialism, check
Russia, and resolve Japan's economic difficulties. The upshot was
the incident at Mukden.

When news of the Mukden affair spread through Japan there
was no rejoicing in the streets, only a popular feeling of satisfaction
that Japanese soldiers were chastising the "upstart" Chinese. Few
people saw that the incident might lead to greater things. In the
government the news brought a shudder. Though not surprised by
the incident (they had suspected that the army might be up to
something in Manchuria), civil leaders dreaded the risks of imperialism. But their position was difficult. The army's action in Manchuria had struck a popular chord at home, and the cabinet felt it
could not afford to appear less patriotic than the army, or less interested in defending Japan's interests in Manchuria. Yale Candee
Maxon in his book *Control of Japanese Foreign Policy* (1957)
chides the civil authorities for their lack of courage: "The results
are a matter of history. By approving the *fait accompli,* the cabinet
lost by default what power it had to shape the course of events and
hastened the approach of the day when the Military would be able
to disregard or dominate it with impunity."

What has been the historical estimate of Japan's action in
Manchuria in 1931?

Among the Japanese the view seems to prevail to the present
day that Japan's economic problems and China's attempt to undermine Japanese interests in Manchuria justified the incident at Mukden and the subsequent Japanese occupation of Manchuria. Japan's
wartime premier, Hideki Tojo, set forth this view at the Tokyo War
Crimes Trial in 1946, and the general-turned-historian, Takushiro
Hattori, reiterated it in his four-volume history of the war in East
Asia (1953). American historians remain unconvinced; their view

is mirrored by Robert Butow, who says simply that "Manchuria was Chinese, and while that did not give the Nationalists [of Chiang Kai-shek] any right to ignore China's treaty obligations toward other powers, neither did geographical propinquity or even special rights and interests confer upon Japan any kind of patent to sever the area from China the moment there was the slightest trouble."

The distinguished Edwin Reischauer (born in Japan of missionary parents, married to a Japanese, and United States ambassador to Japan in the 1960s) declines to accuse or exonerate the Japanese, seeing the entire history of Japanese imperialism in the twentieth century as a tragedy. He explains that Japan's imperial triumphs at the start of the century instilled the dream of rivaling the colonial powers of Europe. Unfortunately the Japanese did not understand that the era of empire-building was already passing, that such powers as Britain and the United States were retreating from their empires and "beginning to abandon the cruder colonial concepts of the nineteenth century." The result was an inevitable clash between Japanese and American interests in East Asia. True, Reischauer continues, Japanese imperial ambition declined in the 1920s. Then came the Great Depression, accompanied by rising tariff barriers in the United States and elsewhere. The Japanese concluded that they must expand or die. Thus they returned to "the game of empire-snatching"—at Mukden in September 1931.

II

Halfway around the world the city of Washington was enduring a hot and humid September. Secretary of State Henry L. Stimson could recall no more discomforting weather since he took office in 1929, and spent numerous evenings fanning himself while sitting under the trees near his white-porticoed mansion. Robert H. Ferrell has written in *American Diplomacy in the Great Depression* (1957) that such weather in those days before air-conditioning made it difficult for the secretary to concentrate on the country's foreign affairs. Besides, the Great Depression had pushed diplomacy to the background of American life. During the previous month, August 1931, one hundred and fifty-eight banks had closed, and in September the rate of bank failures doubled. Unemployment stood between six and ten million. When news began to filter into

Washington about the imbroglio near Mukden there was slight concern. Far more ominous in the American perspective was Britain's departure from the gold standard two days earlier, an event that threatened the shaky foundation of international finance. Unworried over the Manchurian affair, President Hoover and Secretary Stimson left on September 19 for a weekend outing at Hoover's camp on the Rapidan River in Virginia.

Like Washington, the capitals of Europe betrayed no sense of crisis. In London and Paris, as a matter of fact, there was a lot of sympathy for Japan. The British and French had come to admire Japanese industry and efficiency while despising Chinese weakness and disorganization. The British remembered Japan as a faithful ally in the years 1902-22, and saw a parallel between Japan's problem in Manchuria and their own in India. Also, there were signs of increasing Soviet influence in East Asia, and leaders in London envisioned Japan as an Oriental bulwark against communism. The French saw a parallel between their determination to force Germany to abide by the Treaty of Versailles and Japan's determination to compel China to honor treaty commitments. They also saw similarity between their occupation of the Ruhr in Germany in 1923 and Japan's action in Manchuria.

At Geneva the League of Nations reflected the thinking of its leading European members, even when it became clear that Japanese soldiers were operating outside the railway zone. That the affair around Mukden signaled the beginning of the League's decline occurred to no one, and delegates would have been surprised if they could have peered into the future and read historical accounts intimating that in autumn 1931 the League had faced the first serious challenge since its beginning eleven years before. Movement of a few battalions of Japanese infantry in Manchuria hardly bore the markings of a grand military operation. Still, it might be a good idea to investigate, and soon the transatlantic wires were crackling as the League inquired whether the United States would appoint a representative as a member to a Far Eastern investigating commission.

The League's "nagging" and communiqués from China recalling that the United States had sponsored the Kellogg Pact outlawing war forced Secretary Stimson to examine the Manchurian problem. He responded cautiously. The situation in the Far East was opaque; nobody in Europe or America knew what was going on in Manchuria or Tokyo. Stimson knew that Japan had legitimate complaints against China. He also had faith in Japan's civil leaders. Having dealt with them at the London Naval Conference the year before, he respected them and wished them the benefit of every opportunity to get the army under control. Then he had the situation in America to consider. The United States had few interests in Manchuria, the army and navy were weak, the isolationist mood strong, and of course the Depression remained the country's first problem. As for assisting a League of Nations inquiry, Stimson, knowing the anti-League sentiment in the United States, feared the political repercussions of such a close involvement with the world organization.

As days turned into weeks Stimson kept hoping for signs that Japanese troops were retreating to the railway zone, or as he put it, "crawling back into their dens." Unfortunately the Japanese betrayed no intent of returning to the railway zone, and continued to "pursue Chinese bandits" deeper into Manchuria. Then on the morning of October 8 came reports that Japanese planes had bombed the city of Chinchow, many miles from the zone. Shocked, Stimson confided to his diary that "I am afraid we have got to take a firm ground and aggressive stand toward Japan." But firmness and aggression presented as many problems in October as in September. So immersed was the Hoover administration in the economic crisis at home that the President's main purpose in East Asia was not to allow "under any circumstances anybody to deposit that baby in our lap." Stimson concluded that some sort of joint policy with the League might offer the best hope, and persuaded Hoover to authorize an American representative to discuss the situation with the League Council.

The presence of an American delegate at the table of the League Council produced such excitement in Geneva on October 16, 1931 that the United States abruptly backed off again. Hardly had the delegate taken his place —amid exultation by European representatives over the "return of the prodigal son"—before old lines began to re-form in the United States, and such knights of the 1919-20 crusade against the League as Senators Hiram Johnson and William E. Borah were polishing their armor. Stimson, more-over, continued to hope that Japan's civil leaders would assert authority over the military and did not want to endanger America's position as a possible mediator in Manchuria by giving the impression that the United States was joining forces against Japan.

The League labored on, and a week later the Council resolved that Japan must return to the railway zone by November 16. The League then turned its attention across the Atlantic, hoping that the United States would endorse the Council's resolution. It looked in vain. Officers in the State Department were unanimous in their feeling that the time-limit feature of the resolution was a mistake, inasmuch as neither the League nor the United States had the will to give it meaning. They also considered the resolution provocative and likely to strengthen Tokyo's militarists by arousing Japanese patriotism. Still, Stimson felt constrained to lend some support to the League, and on November 5 dispatched a note to Tokyo seeking to "make clear my general support of the League position and yet possibly leave a ladder by which Japan could climb down in case of a deadlock." Though it urged that the Japanese return to the railway zone, the secretary's note contained no time limit.

How does one assess Stimson's policy to this point?

In her book *The Manchurian Crisis, 1931-1932* (1948) Sara R. Smith criticizes the American response to Japan's aggression in autumn 1931. She thinks Japan might have yielded before an American display of force. If Japan had held firm, war would have resulted, but "war in 1931 would have been preferable to war in 1941." Edwin O. Reischauer in *The United States and Japan* takes a similar view: "Japan's one powerful neighbor, immersed in her own compelling economic problems and dominated by a blind belief that she could isolate herself from the problems of the rest of the world, failed to act and by this failure permitted Japan and the world to rush onward toward the catastrophe which was soon to engulf us all."

Few historians agree. Given the Depression, the isolationist mood in the country, and the poor state of America's defenses, Stimson was in no position to take a bellicose stand against the Japanese. In *Henry L. Stimson and Japan, 1931-33* Armin Rappaport writes that "as would any good diplomatist, Stimson was operating within his military capabilities. . . . The Secretary in 1931 had only moral armaments. To have brandished a pistol without having been prepared to shoot would have been a most dangerous policy." Robert H. Ferrell in *American Diplomacy in the Great Depression* says simply that "in retrospect Stimson's caution appears quite sensible and levelheaded."

The League resolution and Stimson note did not bring a ripple of concern from the Japanese, who were busily bringing up infantry, cavalry, artillery, and aircraft against the Chinese. Throughout November 1931 one Manchurian town after another fell to Japanese forces, including the city of Tsitsihar, three hundred and seventy miles north of Mukden. It was clear that Japan had designs on all of Manchuria. As for the civil government, it was powerless to curb the military; indeed, its leaders were living under a threat of assassination. The Manchurian campaign had captured the popular imagination, and—as Rappaport has shown—across Japan shop windows sprouted war maps showing deployment of units, while tea houses buzzed with talk about "our troops" and "the enemy." Stimson recorded in his diary on November 19 that "the Japanese government which we have been dealing with is no longer in control; the situation is in the hands of virtually mad dogs." When the League's deadline for Japan's retreat to the railway zone expired, the government in Tokyo did nothing.

Embarrassed, the League Council revived the idea of an investigating commission. An inquiry would give the appearance that the League was doing something, and might by some miracle open the way for serious negotiation. Pondering the bad press it was beginning to receive, Japan gave its blessing. From Washington the secretary of state tendered American support. Suspecting new Japanese advances in Manchuria, Stimson in truth doubted the inquiry's chances of success. When the League adopted the investigating resolution on December 10 the world sighed in relief. A lull had settled over the frozen Manchurian battlefront, and there was hope, even confidence, that Japan would halt movements in Manchuria pending study by the "Lytton Commission," named for its head, the Earl of Lytton.

The Japanese had no intent of suspending operations during

the League inquiry. A cabinet shuffle took place in Tokyo on December 11, 1931, and next day the new government decided to occupy all of Manchuria. The key to Japanese ambition now became the city of Chinchow, one hundred and seventy-five miles southwest of Mukden. When the Chinese refused Japan's ultimatum to halt "bandit operations" around Chinchow, the Kwantung army on December 23 began to move. Weather was severe, the mercury frequently dropping to twenty degrees below zero, but Japanese soldiers, clad in goatskin jackets, overcoats, and hoods, plodded on. As for the Chinese, their threadbare uniforms mirrored the poverty and weakness of their homeland. Cold, demoralized, and ill-equipped, though greatly outnumbering their enemies, the Chinese fell back, and on January 2, 1932 the Kwantung army entered Chinchow. As the Rising Sun unfurled in the cold Manchurian air Japanese soldiers cheered. The government in Tokyo cheered too, for as Elting E. Morison has written in his biography of Stimson (*Turmoil and Tradition*, 1960): "On that day it was, in effect, master of Manchuria."

In Washington, Stimson, reading dispatches, was furious, and his temperature went higher when the chief of the State Department's Far Eastern Division compared Chinchow with the last dish in a set of dishes: Stimson had watched Japan break dish after dish. Why should he be so angry when Japan broke the last dish? After calming down the secretary decided that the cautious policy of the previous months was futile. Toughness would be the new line.

Pondering alternatives, Stimson saw immediately that isolationist sentiment and military weakness ruled out intervention by American forces. But what about an economic blockade, or sanctions? Japanese industry depended on American oil and cotton, and Japan sold a third of its exports in the United States. Sanctions by the United States would bring Japan's Depression-laden economy to ruin. Surely leaders in Tokyo would give up aggression before letting sanctions be brought to bear. Sanctions, of course, were risky. The Japanese might retaliate and entangle the United States in war. Then Japan was one of America's best customers, no small consideration in the Depression.

Another obstacle was the President. Several weeks earlier Hoover, a peaceful man, had made it clear that he did not like the idea of sanctions, telling a cabinet meeting that "we will not go along on any of the sanctions, either economic or military, for these are roads to war." Chinchow brought no change in Hoover's view. He still refused to indulge in "sticking pins in tigers."

The differences between Hoover and Stimson on the question of sanctions have stirred some historical controversy. Asserting that "my able Secretary was at times more of a warrior than a diplomat," Hoover in the first volume of his memoirs (*The Cabinet and the Presidency*, 1951) indicated a sharp division between the two men: "To him [Stimson] the phrase 'economic sanctions' (boycott) was the magic wand of force by which all peace could be summoned from the vasty deep." The historian Richard N. Current strikes a similar chord in an article, "The Stimson Doctrine and the Hoover Doctrine" (*American Historical Review*, LIX, 1953-54). Largely on the basis of references in the diaries of Stimson and Assistant Secretary of State William R. Castle to the possibility of an economic boycott of Japan, he concludes that the idea of sanctions became increasingly attractive to Stimson. When Hoover held out against sanctions, Current thinks, a rift developed between the President and his secretary of state.

Robert H. Ferrell in *American Diplomacy in the Great Depression* takes a different view. Though he concedes that the idea of sanctions appealed to Stimson, he maintains that after outbursts of anger against the Japanese—which usually preceded random diary remarks about sanctions—the secretary would realize that domestic political considerations ruled out the possibility of economic coercion. Contrary to Current, Ferrell thinks Hoover and Stimson agreed more than they disagreed on Far Eastern policy in 1931-32.

Stimson's memoirs (*On Active Service*, 1947) seem to reinforce Ferrell's observations. Admitting that he "had argued with Mr. Hoover several times" about sanctions, Stimson did not intimate that the subject was a source of serious disagreement. Indeed, he went out of his way to emphasize that in opposing sanctions "Mr. Hoover was squarely in line with the whole tradition of American foreign policy in the Far East" and in 1931-32 "was traveling in company with most of his countrymen."

Elting Morison in his biography of Stimson takes a position

somewhere between the two. Like Ferrell, he does not think there was a serious dispute between Hoover and Stimson over the application of sanctions. An economic boycott of Japan was out of the question and both men knew it. But Morison believes they differed rather heatedly on the desirability of issuing an announcement that the United States would not impose sanctions. According to Morison, Stimson thought an announcement "would take from him a threat he believed he could use to coerce the Japanese." But Hoover, "to avoid frightening Japan into a war," wanted to reassure the leaders in Tokyo (and eventually did).

III

Blocked in the matter of sanctions, Stimson in January 1932 turned to nonrecognition of Japan's conquest, an idea Hoover had mentioned in a cabinet meeting the previous November. If supported by many other countries, nonrecognition would demonstrate the world's outrage at Japan's adventure. It would also preclude treaties or other diplomatic arrangements regarding Manchuria, making the hazards of doing business there so great that European and American capitalists might shy away. Such moral and economic pressure hopefully would bring the Japanese to the conference table. Nonrecognition of course had the advantage of involving no risk of armed retaliation by Japan, for it implied no follow-up by force.

Stimson took his thoughts on nonrecognition to Hoover, who was still occupied by domestic economic problems. The President urged him to apply the policy. The result was a note handed to the Japanese ambassador on January 7, 1932 proclaiming a policy that would take Stimson's name into history. Known as the Stimson Doctrine, the policy announced that the United States would not recognize the legality of any treaty situation *de facto* in the Far East that impaired the treaty rights of the United States or its citizens in China, violated the Open Door, or came about in violation of the Kellogg-Briand Pact.[1]

The success of nonrecognition depended on support by other powers, notably Britain and France. Though he had not consulted

---

[1] An identical note went to China, a perfunctory step inasmuch as the Chinese were threatening no American treaty rights.

British or French leaders before issuing the note of January 7, Stimson expected them to "repair to the standard." He felt particularly confident of support from London. His confidence was ill-founded. Britain's main concern was commercial equality in Manchuria, repeatedly promised them by the Japanese after the Mukden incident. The London government had no interest in futile moral pronouncements that might impair trade. The British were also thinking of their holdings in the Far East—Hong Kong, Malaya, Burma—and saw Japan as a threat. Arousing the Japanese against the British Empire by lining up with the Stimson Doctrine would not be very smart. Britain's conservative circles also admired Japan's imperial tradition, feared Soviet expansion in East Asia, and felt that Britain had erred in 1922 in breaking the twenty-year-old alliance with Japan in the name of Anglo-American friendship. The French held similar views; and specifically that so long as the Japanese remained occupied in Manchuria they would not turn attention to the French colony of Indochina (present-day Vietnam, Laos, and Cambodia). In a few days, therefore, it became apparent that Britain and France would not support the nonrecognition doctrine. The American secretary of state had failed to touch diplomatic bases, moved out in front of world opinion, and as one correspondent put it, the United States was left "holding the sack."

The moral tone of Stimson's nonrecognition note may have been pleasing to Americans, but its only consequence was to rouse Japanese hostility against the United States. From Tokyo came a reply to the note that fairly reeked with cynicism. Regarding the Kellogg-Briand Pact, the Japanese said: "It might be the subject of an academic doubt whether in a given case the impropriety of means necessarily and always voids the ends secured; but as Japan has no intention of adopting improper means, the question does not practically arise." Referring to the Nine-Power Treaty of 1922 in which Japan had pledged to respect the territory of China, also mentioned in Stimson's note, the Japanese declared that "the present unsettled and distracted state of China is not what was in the contemplation of the high contracting parties at the time of the Treaty of Washington." The note concluded with an insolent reminder that the United States itself had played the imperial game in the Pacific a generation before when it took Hawaii and the Philippines.

Hardly had Stimson absorbed Tokyo's rebuff when the Japanese assaulted China's largest port, Shanghai. To anxious diplomats across the world this affair, begun in the last days of January 1932, looked like the second phase in a grand design to subjugate China. Diplomatic guessing was wrong, however, for the Shanghai incident was the work of an obscure rear admiral in charge of Japan's naval contingent at the port, and occurred to the embarrassment of the government in Tokyo. Only when they concluded that national prestige was committed did Japanese authorities enlarge the operation.

Secretary Stimson saw the attack at Shanghai as being as evil as Germany's invasion of Belgium in 1914, and recalled "how outraged we were when President Wilson did nothing to show the shame that we felt." He wanted to make a show of force by moving the Asiatic fleet from Manila to Shanghai. Hoover, in no mood for bluffs, refused consent. Stimson next proposed an international conference under the Nine-Power Treaty. Such a conference would require British support, and when that government turned down the idea he concluded that the British were "soft" and "pudgy," "very cold-footed." The secretary then decided to make another moral pronouncement. But he did not want to express his thoughts in a speech. "The British have pocketed me on the note method of doing it," he confided to his diary, and "I do not dare to send a note on the Nine-Power Treaty for fear of the yellow-bellied responses that I will get from some of the countries." He settled for another unilateral declaration, similar to the nonrecognition note of January 7 but more dramatic. He arrived at the idea of his newest missive while on a morning horseback ride in Rock Creek Park: he would write a public letter to Chairman William E. Borah of the Senate Foreign Relations Committee.

Stimson sent his letter to Borah on February 23, 1932. Like the Stimson Doctrine note, it reaffirmed American rights in the Far East. It also contained a veiled threat that further Japanese aggression might cause the United States to reconsider pledges made in 1922 not to enlarge fortifications in Guam and the Philippines and (in the Five-Power Treaty) to limit naval tonnage. Such a threat amounted to bluff. There was no chance that President Hoover or Congress would approve new fortifications at Pacific bases or set aside restrictions on naval armament.

Bluffed or not, the Japanese soon decided to abandon the Shanghai operation. The great port at the mouth of the Yangtze was not yet an object of Japanese imperial policy. The affair, moreover, was taking much national energy, delaying consolidation of the Manchurian conquest, and bringing bad publicity. After achieving sufficient success to salvage their military reputation the Japanese indicated their willingness to negotiate the Shanghai problem. An armistice was reached in May 1932.

As for the historical verdict on Stimson's nonrecognition policy, the prevailing view has been that the policy was badly conceived. A few years after the Manchurian crisis, in 1938, A. Whitney Griswold (*The Far Eastern Policy of the United States*) wrote that unilateral pronouncements condemning Japan "left the United States to bear the brunt of a Japanese antagonism that Stimson's discreet European collaborators were altogether happy to avoid." Writing in 1963, Armin Rappaport (*Henry L. Stimson and Japan*) expressed a similar view when he said that Stimson "elected to give vent to his ire by brandishing the pistol, which, unhappily, was not loaded, thereby transgressing the cardinal maxim of the statesman and placing his country in jeopardy." A more rancorous expression of the same view appeared in Charles C. Tansill's *Back Door to War* (1952). Tansill describes the nonrecognition doctrine as "a bomb whose long fuse sputtered dangerously for several years and finally burst into the flame of World War II." He sees irony in Stimson's position as secretary of war in President Franklin D. Roosevelt's cabinet at the time of Pearl Harbor, saying, "no one deserved that title quite as well as he."

Tansill also strongly phrases a second criticism of Stimson's Far Eastern policy: that the secretary failed to give proper consideration to Soviet ambition in East Asia. Regarding the Japanese empire as a bastion against communist expansion in East Asia, Tansill presents the Japanese as reasonable people pursuing legitimate ends but constantly forced to more bellicose stands by the shortsighted and self-righteous secretary of state. Had Stimson been more alert to reality he would have seen that the Japanese, by throwing up a bulwark against the Soviets, were defending America against the menace of international communism.

Though he makes no attempt to cloak Japanese imperialism in sweet reasonableness, and takes care not to reproach Stimson, the historian-diplomat George F. Kennan also thinks the United States should have recognized the Japanese as an instrument for containing communism in East Asia. In *American Diplomacy, 1900-1950* (1951) he explains that the "legalistic-moralistic" policy in Manchuria set the United States on a course hostile to any Japanese influence in that area. Such a policy ignored Chinese weakness and historic Russian ambition: "Today we have fallen heir to the problems and responsibilities the Japanese had faced and borne in the Korean-Manchurian area for nearly half a century, and there is a certain perverse justice in the pain we are suffering from a burden which, when it was borne by others, we held in such low esteem."

Richard N. Current takes a similar view in his essay "Henry L. Stimson" (Norman A. Graebner, ed., *An Uncertain Tradition,* 1961), asserting that Stimson was a lawyer who, when in the State Department, took an attorney's approach to international conflicts: "The law was the law. There was a right and a wrong in every case. Trespassers must be prosecuted." Current writes that the Japanese, and the Germans as well, had legitimate grievances against existing international arrangements, but Stimson made himself a defender of the *status quo*. One wonders if Current, and others who have expressed similar ideas, have not become captives of their own rhetoric (for it is hard to write about Stimson without dwelling on his stern demeanor and uncompromising sense of duty and morality). At the time of the Mukden incident Stimson did not burst forth with pronouncements that Japan had broken the law. Sympathetic toward Japan, he moved cautiously. There is nothing in the record to indicate that he would have opposed renegotiation of Japan's treaty arrangements in Manchuria. Only after the Japanese made clear their intent to grab all of Manchuria and sever it from China did his position harden.

In his full-dress biography of Stimson, *Turmoil and Tradition,* Elting E. Morison takes a more tolerant view of Stimson's diplomacy. He recognizes the futility of the Far Eastern policy, saying that Stimson "wound up like a man before a breaking dam with a shovel in his hands." Still, he thinks the secretary "left behind an image in the public mind, the image of a man in a time when the maximum effort was nowhere put forward who would do with all his might what there was left to do."

Then there is Robert H. Ferrell, the scholar who has studied Stimson's secretaryship in greatest depth. Expressing respect for Kennan's criticism, Ferrell writes in *American Diplomacy in the Great Depression* that there is something to say for Stimson's tactics: "The moral approach to foreign policy is rooted deeply in the traditions and thoughts of Western civilization, particularly in the main current of American democratic thought." He believes that Stimson's critics have attacked the moral approach because of the impossibility of its complete success, overlooking the absence of an acceptable substitute. He also thinks "morality in politics, a noble goal well worth striving for, has in addition a certain practical use in the workaday politics of democratic nations."

One must conclude that it is possible to make a case against Stimson's Far Eastern policy. The policy exacerbated relations between the United States and Japan, moved the countries toward war, failed to consider ancient Russian ambition in Manchuria and Korea, did not face the question of Manchuria's fate in event of Japanese expulsion from the area. One can also make a case for the secretary's attempt to uphold international morality. Should Stimson have closed his eyes to Japanese attacks on the Chinese? Should he have uttered no protest while Japan trampled on the treaties of 1922 and 1928 and led the world back to jungle law? What are treaties for? In his memoirs (*On Active Service*) Stimson recalled that he had told the cabinet that the Japanese "are parties to these treaties and the whole world looks on to see whether the treaties are good for anything or not, and if we lie down and treat them like scraps of paper nothing will happen, and in the future the peace movement will receive a blow that it will not recover from for a long time." Ignoring Japan's treaty violations, he wrote in 1947, "was unthinkable. Whatever they might be to other statesmen or to other nations, the treaties were not scraps of paper. . . . Respect for treaties was the very foundation of peace."

Still, one wonders whether Stimson's vision of the national interest was as hazy as critics have thought—whether his moralizing did not have a larger purpose than upholding the sanctity of treaties and proclaiming America's righteousness. When he pondered America's problem in the Far East, Stimson did not dwell on communism or the chances of war with Japan. He focused on China. In *The Far Eastern Crisis,* published in 1936, he wrote that "the future of the Far East will be very largely dominated by the future of the four hundred fifty million people of Chinese blood." As if peering into the 1960s, he said that "if the character of China should be revolutionized and through exploitation become militaristic and aggressive, not only Asia but the rest of the world must tremble." Thus a central object of Stimson's policy was to assure the friendship of the slumbering giant of East Asia. Who is to say after the past twenty years that such an objective was wrongheaded? As the twentieth century progresses, historians may look back and proclaim that the tragedy of our time was the failure of Western leaders to accept Stimson's analysis and bend heaven and earth to build a peaceful China.

The Japanese meanwhile had tightened their grip on Manchuria, and early in 1932 were wrestling with the political future of the territory. They decided to make it an independent country bound to Japan. To make the new state seem Chinese, they determined to revive the Manchu dynasty, which had been evicted from Peking in 1911. Fortunately the Manchu "boy emperor" had survived the 1911-12 revolution and was living in Tientsin under the name of Henry Pu Yi. After a fast journey by automobile, train, and boat to Mukden, Pu Yi agreed to act as regent in the new kingdom. Japan then pressed on with plans for an independent state. Named Manchukuo, the new country made its appearance in March 1932. Its national emblem consisted of the five bars of the old flag of Imperial China, emblazoned with Japan's rising sun.

Hoping that such powers as Britain and France would recognize the new regime first, the Tokyo government delayed its own formal recognition. Then came frustration. The Assembly of the League of Nations, dominated by less powerful countries (more sensitive than the great powers to the danger of aggression going unpunished), began to discuss the possibility of sanctions against Japan under Article XVI of the League Covenant. Lest the Assembly embroil the League in a Far Eastern war, Britain and France jumped into the debate and in March 1932 persuaded the Assembly as a compromise to endorse the American policy of refusing to recognize Japan's conquest of Manchuria.

While the Japanese fumed, the Lytton Commission quietly went about gathering information on the Manchurian affair. After spending time in Japan, China, and Manchuria interviewing officials, taking testimony, and visiting sites, the commission wrote its report. The Lytton report took note of China's efforts to destroy Japan's treaty-protected sphere of interest, but insisted that Japan's response to the events of September 1931 had far exceeded Chinese provocation. As for Manchukuo, the report called the new country a Japanese creation, and declared that recognition of its government would violate international obligations set forth in the Nine-Power and Kellogg-Briand treaties. The commission recommended an autonomous Manchurian regime within the Chinese Republic, demilitarization, and a guarantee of Japanese treaty rights in the area. Although the Tokyo government already had recognized Manchukuo, hope was widespread that Japan might accept the Lytton report's recommendations. Such hope was vain. The Japanese had put too much blood and toil into the Manchurian venture.

As the League wrung its hands, Secretary Stimson insisted that Japan should not go uncensured. President Hoover's defeat in the national election of November 1932 weakened Stimson's hand, but early in 1933 President-elect Roosevelt endorsed Stimson's Far Eastern policies. The League, over the opposition of conservatives in Britain and France (Winston Churchill said that "we do not want to throw away our old valued friendship with Japan"), adopted the Lytton report. At that point, in February 1933, the Japanese delegation stalked out of the League. The chief delegate, Yosuke Matsuoka, told reporters that as Christ was crucified on the cross, so the League had crucified Japan. Passing through the United States on his way home he explained that the powers of

Europe had taught Japan the game of poker, but after acquiring most of the chips they had pronounced the game immoral and taken up contract bridge.

Among those who watched the drama of Japan's exit from the League was the American minister at Geneva, Hugh R. Wilson. In his memoir *Diplomat Between Wars* (1941) Wilson recalled that at that moment he had begun to wonder whether the course he and his colleagues had been following had been wrong. He suspected that if nations felt strong enough to condemn they ought to feel strong enough to apply force. It occurred to him that condemnation created a community of the damned whose members one day might come together against their accusers. Wilson wrote that when he left the Assembly chamber he was troubled as never before.

On leaving the League the Japanese enlarged their Chinese acquisitions, taking Jehol province in North China early in 1933. With that conquest their appetite for territory was temporarily satisfied. Both the military and civil members of the government accepted what the army had taken, and agreed to no further conquest. The hostilities between Japan and China, never formally declared, came to a temporary end on May 31, 1933, when officials of the two governments met at the town of Tangku near the Great Wall. After humiliating Chinese delegates by forcing them to leave their special train and walk across a dusty roadway to the Japanese barracks, Tokyo's negotiators accepted a truce.

THREE

Dictators and Neutrality

While the Japanese were devouring Manchuria, trouble was appearing in another corner of the world: in central Europe, Germany's republican government, torn by dissension and weighted down by economic problems, had begun its death agony. If few Germans mourned the passing of republicanism, many felt foreboding, for Germany was echoing to a chorus of conflicting voices and above the din there rang stentorian calls to violence. At the center of the national confusion—and urging it on—were the political extremists, communists on the left and National Socialists (Nazis) on the right, and throughout 1932 the two parties struggled over Germany's political wreckage. As the country edged toward chaos many Germans looked to the relic of the 1914-18 war, the president of the Republic, Paul von Hindenburg. There was no easy solution to Germany's political problems, but when he pondered the situation the aging president decided that he liked communists less than Nazis, and to head off the former appointed the National Socialist leader, Adolf Hitler, as chancellor.

It was January 1933.

Hindenburg's act boded ill for the world, but neither he nor outsiders dreamed what the next dozen years would bring. Such ignorance had little excuse, for Hitler had been spelling out his aims for ten years or more. In foreign affairs he would reassert German power, recover "lost" territories, expand the national borders to provide *lebensraum* for the German people. When he gained power in 1933 this dark, brooding, Wagnerian German determined to fulfill his vision to the last detail.

To the south of Germany, in Italy, another "strong man" had appeared, Benito Mussolini, and by the 1930s he too had thoughts of expansion. An adventure in imperialism would solve Italy's problem of surplus population, prove its greatness as a nation, and enhance its influence and prestige in the world.

I

While Hitler was consolidating power in Germany, Americans early in 1933 awaited a new presidential administration. They waited in an atmosphere of frustration and despair, for the Great Depression had reached its nadir. The change in national leadership came on March 4, when Franklin D. Roosevelt, smiling and waving, drove up Pennsylvania Avenue to the Capitol and took the oath as thirty-second President of the American Republic. After telling his countrymen that they had nothing to fear except fear, he set in motion an unprecedented program, the New Deal, to relieve victims of the Depression and find a way to recovery. As for foreign affairs, the historian Samuel Flagg Bemis has written (preface to Volume XII, *The American Secretaries of State and Their Diplomacy,* 1964) that "nobody in 1933 expected there would be any great problems of diplomacy; it was enough to be a good neighbor to all nations."

Two questions in diplomacy nonetheless demanded attention:

the World Disarmament Conference meeting at Geneva and the World Economic Conference scheduled to open a few months later in London. Convened in spring 1932, the disarmament conference by spring 1933 was mired in France's fears of Germany. The French remembered how in 1870 and again in 1914 German armies had pressed toward Paris, and refused to consider disarmament without guarantees of support in event of a new German attack. Roosevelt and his secretary of state, Cordell Hull of Tennessee, sympathized with France, but America's isolationist mood prevented them from making adequate assurances. As for the new German chancellor, he seemed conciliatory, indicating that he would wait five years before insisting on equality in arms, and when the British offered a plan for disarming that included clauses for collective action against aggressors the prospects for an agreement seemed to brighten. Then came one of the darkest days of the 1930s. On October 14, 1933, Hitler's government announced that it was withdrawing from the Geneva conference and quitting the League of Nations. Without Germany there was no chance for disarmament.

Plans for American participation in a world economic conference had matured under President Hoover, and when Roosevelt entered the White House in March 1933 the meeting was set for the following June in London. The conference hopefully would stabilize world currencies and revive international trade. Such aims were in harmony with the ideas of Secretary of State Hull, who saw trade barriers as the largest obstacle to peace, and with enthusiasm he sailed off to London as head of the American delegation. Disappointment awaited the secretary, for by June 1933 Roosevelt was having new thoughts about the conference. Thanks to inflationary fiscal policies of the previous two months the American economy had taken a sharp turn upward. Further tinkering with the national monetary system might help it to recover further. Hence the President was reluctant to stabilize the dollar at the present level. Roosevelt also suspected Britain and France of seeking an arrangement that would work to their special advantage. The result was his "bombshell" message of early July 1933 rejecting the conference's ideas on stabilization, rapping delegates for giving currency questions a higher priority than other "fundamental ills," and proclaiming his view that planned national currencies were superior to "old fetishes of the so-called international bankers." Without American support discussion was useless, and the conference adjourned a short time later.

Asserting that "the President's mischievous message destroyed the conference," the historian William E. Leuchtenburg (*Franklin D. Roosevelt and the New Deal,* 1963) has written that "there is probably no act of Roosevelt's White House years for which he has been more universally censured." Leuchtenburg is among the critics, stating that the United States, "as the most powerful nation in the world, and as the principal creditor, . . . had a special obligation to lead." He says the London conference "marked the last opportunity of democratic statesmen to work out a co-operative solution to common economic problems," and that "the collapse of the conference sapped the morale of the democratic opponents of fascism."

Broadus Mitchell and Cordell Hull have expressed similar ideas. In his book *Depression Decade* (1947) Mitchell wonders if "Roosevelt did not contribute heavily to the international and political deterioration that led to fresh war." Many years after the conference Hull wrote (*Memoirs of Cordell Hull,* 1948) that during the London meeting "the dictator nations occupied front-row seats at a spectacular battle" between "the peace-keeping nations." With collapse of the conference "they could proceed hopefully: on the military side, to rearm in comparative safety; on the economic side, to build their self-sufficiency walls in preparation for war." Hull concluded, as Leuchtenburg also did fifteen years later, that "the conference was the first, and really the last, opportunity to check these movements toward conflict."

The distinguished historian-diplomat Herbert Feis, an adviser to the American delegation at the London meeting, declines in his book *1933: Characters in Crisis* (1966) to attack the President and stops short of any judgment about the part played by the conference in the collapse of peace in the 1930s. Still, it is clear that Feis thinks Roosevelt erred in taking action that brought an end to the London discussions, and in his epilogue chides the President for his determination in 1933 to avoid any responsibility for guarding peace.

Other writers have disputed the idea that the London conference might have succeeded if Roosevelt had not interfered, and hence have absolved the President, at least in this instance, of taking action that opened the way for the aggression of Hitler and Mussolini. Julius W. Pratt in his study *Cordell Hull* (Volumes XII and XIII in *The American Secretaries of State and Their Diplomacy*, 1964) argues that "the best opinion a quarter-century later held that even without Roosevelt's controversial manifesto, the Conference had little prospect of agreeing on a solution for any major problems." Selig Adler (*The Uncertain Giant*, 1965) agrees: "In retrospect, the tragedy lay not in the Roosevelt message which undermined the Conference, but in an all-pervading selfish nationalism which ruled a mutual recovery program out of the realm of political possibilities." Arthur M. Schlesinger, Jr., (*The Age of Roosevelt*, Volume III, *The Coming of the New Deal*, 1959) blames the "gold-standard approach to London" for failure of the conference (France in particular wanted to restore the international gold standard), stating "it can be said that it could not conceivably have produced agreement." And Paul K. Conkin in *The New Deal* (1967), a volume in the *Crowell American History Series*, says simply that "the tasks of the conference were . . . surely impossible."

The darkening state of world politics in the early 1930s caused some Americans to feel that it was time to revise the country's neutrality laws. America's stance when other countries went to war was not a new subject, and most of the arguments had appeared in other years. In sum, individuals who believed that no "foreign" war concerned the United States wanted legislation designed to prevent a collision with belligerents—as in 1915-17 when ships carrying supplies from America to Britain and France became targets of German submarines. (A classroom witticism of the present day is that isolationists of the 1930s wanted laws to keep the United States out of the war of 1914-18.) The isolationist prescription was alluringly simple: at the onset of war anywhere in the world the United States should simply terminate trade with the belligerents.

An economic boycott of this kind raised problems, however. Could the United States in good conscience deny food and medical supplies to civilians of belligerent countries? There also was the effect of a total embargo on the American economy to consider, no small matter in the Depression. Aware of the complexities they faced, isolationists concentrated on embargoes limited to arms and ammunition. The idea of an arms embargo had special appeal to Americans of the 1930s, many of whom were anxious to strike at munitions makers, the awful "merchants of death" who took profit from war.

Isolationist arguments met sharp opposition. Some people saw embargoes that fell impartially on all belligerents, victims and aggressors alike, as a cowardly policy that did violence to the spirit of the Kellogg Pact. Others thought that twentieth-century technology had dated nineteenth-century ideas of isolation, that the United States could no longer escape a general war. These anti-isolationists talked of laws permitting the President to close American ports to peace-breakers. Putting aggressor nations on notice that only their victims would receive nourishment from America, such measures might deter war. Failing that, they would enable the United States to take collective action with other countries, perhaps the League of Nations, to nip aggression and prevent the spread of war.

Isolationists recoiled at the idea of discriminating between belligerents. How could the President be sure which side was the aggressor? War was complicated, and as scholarly debate over the origins of the World War had shown, it was hard to be sure even a generation later who was guilty. To make an accurate judgment amid the confusions of an exploding conflict probably would be difficult, and if the President erred the consequences might be tragic. Even supposing he correctly ascertained which was the guilty party, might not the designated aggressor retaliate? Retaliation would mean American involvement in the war.

There was, one should add, a middle group that wanted no change in existing neutrality law. Many proponents of the *status quo* represented business interests and wanted no interference, by embargo or otherwise, if an overseas war presented opportunity for increased trade. Others were individuals who felt strongly about the principles of international law and argued that it would be a shameful abandonment of freedom of the seas if, as isolationists wanted, the United States announced upon the outbreak of war that it was leaving the international waterways to belligerents. As for discriminatory embargoes, they were unduly provocative.

II

The shadow of war began to lengthen in December 1934 when Italian and Ethiopian troops clashed at Ualual on the Ethiopian-Somaliland frontier in East Africa. Intent on conquest, the Italians refused a peaceful settlement, and the result was a quarrel that smoldered through spring and summer 1935. To the north there were equally ominous disturbances. Following an intensive Nazi propaganda campaign the people of the mineral-rich Saar Basin, acting under the Treaty of Versailles (1919), voted in January 1935 for union with Germany. Two months later Hitler renounced the disarmament provisions of the Versailles arrangement, putting the world on notice that Germany was planning a military renaissance.

In America meanwhile the neutrality debate reached Capitol Hill, and before the end of summer 1935 Congress passed new neutrality legislation.

The previous September (1934) the Senate's Special Committee Investigating the Munitions Industry had begun hearings under the chairmanship of Senator Gerald P. Nye of North Dakota (see Chapter One), and for several weeks newspapers across the world bannered the committee's revelations about the "merchants of death." After a lapse the committee resumed hearings in February 1935, and for two months studied activities of the shipbuilding industry (collusive bidding for the navy's ships was the main charge against shipbuilders) and assorted proposals for mobilizing the American economy in time of war to restrict profit and "equalize burdens." There were no hearings on neutrality. In spring 1935, however, committee investigators began to gather material concerning American entry into the World War in 1917 (the basis of hearings on the subject of neutrality in January-February 1936), Senator Nye began to speak out about the need for America to isolate itself from foreign quarrels, and in June 1935 Nye and his Munitions Committee colleague, Senator Bennett Champ Clark of Missouri, introduced bills for an impartial arms embargo against belligerents, a prohibition on loans to belligerents, and denial of passports to Americans wishing to enter war zones.

Noting that neutrality legislation came (August 1935) directly in the wake of the "Nye Committee" hearings—and also noting that Nye and such committee stalwarts as Clark, Homer T. Bone of Washington, and Arthur H. Vandenberg of Michigan were in the van of those urging isolation—numerous writers have given the arms inquiry much credit for the neutrality law's passage. Dexter Perkins (*The New Age of Franklin Roosevelt*, 1957) sees the Nye Committee as encouraging an isolationist spirit in 1934-35 by advancing "the thesis that American entry into the [World] war was the work of wicked Wall Street bankers, aided and abetted by sinister arms barons." Thomas A. Bailey (*The Man in the Street: The Impact of Public Opinion on Foreign Policy*, 1948) says the committee aroused the public "over the wrong things, and this state of mind contributed powerfully to the passage of the heads-in-the-sands neutrality legislation of the 1930's." In his memoirs Cordell Hull charges that "the Nye Committee aroused an isolationist sentiment that was to tie the hands of the Administration just at the very time when our hands should have been free to place the weight of our influence in the scales where it would count." Charles A. Beard has written (*America in Midpassage*, 1939) that "the Nye committee's findings spread distrust of presidential discretion in handling foreign affairs and stimulated the popular interest that culminated in the neutrality legislation of 1935." In the first volume of his memoirs (*Year of Decisions*, 1955) Harry S. Truman writes that "this committee made it appear that the munitions manufacturers had caused World War I, and as a result, the Neutrality Act was passed." The historians Selig Adler (*The Isolationist Impulse*, 1957) and Robert A. Divine (*The Illusion of Neutrality*, 1962) have also observed a close connection between the munitions inquiry and the neutrality legislation, and Wayne S. Cole in his excellent book *Senator Gerald P. Nye and American Foreign Relations* (1962) writes that "without the Nye committee the neutrality laws probably would not have been adopted by Congress."

In my book *In Search of Peace: The Senate Munitions Inquiry, 1934-36* (1963) I conclude that most writers have exaggerated the responsibility of the Nye investigation for the isolationist neutrality law of 1935. Before passage of the legislation the Munitions Committee held no hearings and made no revelations regarding neutrality (these did not occur until January 1936).

Until summer 1935 it took no positions that one could term isolationist, and indeed had enjoyed wide support of "internationalists," including James P. Pope of Idaho, a member of the committee and perhaps the Senate's most outspoken advocate of collective security. It is possible that by talking so much about peace the committee unwittingly helped create a climate favorable to isolationist neutrality legislation, and that publicity generated by the inquiry strengthened the position of such isolationists as Nye and Clark during the neutrality debate in Congress. Still, it seems to me that the weakening of peace in Europe, and specifically the collapse of Italo-Ethiopian negotiations, were chiefly responsible for the neutrality law of 1935.

Whatever the reasons, Congress in summer 1935 became increasingly interested in American policy during foreign wars, and as mentioned Senators Nye and Clark introduced isolationist measures. The Roosevelt administration, opposed to "mandatory" isolation, countered with a bill that would permit discriminatory embargoes. The bill found little response. Chairman Key Pittman of the Senate Foreign Relations Committee told presidential secretary Stephen Early: "I tell you, Steve, the President is riding for a fall if he insists on designating the aggressor in accordance with the wishes of the League of Nations. . . . I will introduce it [a discretionary bill] on behalf of the Administration without comment, but he will be licked as sure as hell." There is no assurance, of course, that Roosevelt would have used the authority granted in a discretionary bill to co-operate with the League or punish aggression, for he was not an advocate of collective security in the present-day sense. Wishing to retain the executive's freedom to maneuver in foreign affairs, he wanted legislation that would enable him to pursue isolation, punish aggressors, co-operate with the League, or do nothing.

It appeared in mid-August that there would be no neutrality legislation in 1935. Then came dispatches from Paris (August 19) revealing that negotiations between Ethiopia and Italy had collapsed. As gloom settled over Washington isolationists in the Senate threatened a filibuster against the adjournment of Congress unless an isolationist measure passed. Exhausted by the summer's heat, the Foreign Relations Committee reported a joint resolution prohibiting export of munitions to belligerents after the President declared the existence of war, restricting use of American ports by belligerent submarines, and authorizing the President to proclaim that Americans traveling on ships of belligerent registry did so at their own risk. Deferring to the country's rampaging isolationism, the administration reluctantly permitted the bill to pass, but won an amendment limiting it to six months.

When East Africa's rainy season ended early in October 1935, Mussolini's armies attacked and Roosevelt invoked the Neutrality Act. A fortnight later the League, showing more backbone than it had in the Manchurian affair, named Italy an aggressor and voted sanctions. Because of America's obsession with impartiality toward belligerents there was little that Roosevelt and Hull could do to support the League action. Their only option was an expedient dubbed a "moral embargo." Announcing that abnormal trade with belligerents in nonmilitary commodities (not covered by the Neutrality Act) violated the spirit of the recent legislation, they urged Americans to limit commerce with East Africa's belligerents to "peacetime levels." As Brice Harris, Jr., explains in *The United States and the Italo-Ethiopian Crisis* (1964), "because there was little actual or potential trade with Ethiopia," the more the administration "limited trade with belligerents, the more it was co-operating with the League of Nations in imposing economic sanctions on Italy." American businessmen, however, refused to support the moral embargo, and through winter 1935-36 the Atlantic churned with freighters and tankers carrying scrap metal, oil, and cotton to Italian ports.

Congress reconvened in January 1936 and neutrality again was an issue, for the legislation enacted the previous August would expire on February 29. Senator Nye's committee by now was spotlighting neutrality, and isolationist members hoped to win support for total embargoes—with revelations that business with the Allies had taken the United States into the World War. They hoped in vain. Though the committee exhibited strong evidence that trade with the Allies in 1914-17 had made the United States an object of German strategy, most members of Congress refused to go beyond arms embargoes. President Roosevelt also was making plans. He hoped that new legislation would leave some room for discriminating between belligerents, and his neutrality proposal included cleverly worded sections designed to give the President limited control over export of nonmilitary commodities. The proposal got nowhere.

Since the expiration of the 1935 law was drawing near, a move began in February 1936 for enacting the old legislation. The administration fell in line, and Senator Nye's more extreme isolationists, after considering a filibuster, gave up on total embargoes. The result was the Neutrality Act of 1936, identical to the 1935 law except for a few amendments, the most important of which forbade Americans to lend money to belligerents, a concession to the Nye group. Like the previous act, the new one was temporary and would expire on May 1, 1937.

III

Overseas the situation continued to worsen. Hitler's troops entered the demilitarized zones of the Rhineland in March 1936 in violation of the Versailles Treaty. Two months later, after the fall of Addis Ababa, Italy annexed Ethiopia and quit the League of Nations. Civil war broke out in Spain in July. The following autumn Germany and Italy announced the "Rome-Berlin axis" and Germany and Japan signed the Anti-Comintern Pact against Russia, which Italy joined the next year.

The State Department meanwhile set out to broaden the Good Neighbor policy in the interest of hemispheric solidarity—to strengthen the New World against outside aggression by committing every country in the Western Hemisphere to the nonintervention principle of the Monroe Doctrine. In pursuit of the policy the Washington government in 1936 engineered a special Inter-American Conference "to determine how the maintenance of peace among the American Republics may best be safeguarded." To encourage the conference Roosevelt, shortly after winning re-election in November 1936, sailed to Buenos Aires as "a traveling salesman of peace" and addressed the opening session. When he met an enthusiastic reception it seemed that hemispheric solidarity was at hand. But no agreement followed.

A more urgent matter was the Spanish civil war. The American government in August 1936 reinforced an agreement among Europe's powers to keep clear of the conflict by announcing a "moral embargo" on arms shipments to Spain. To make the policy effective Congress in January 1937, on Roosevelt's recommendation, voted an arms embargo against both sides in the civil war. Julius W. Pratt has written (*Cordell Hull*) that the policy pleased isolationists "because it kept the United States aloof from the conflict, internationalists because it meant co-operation with France and England." Then Hitler and Mussolini threw their weight behind General Francisco Franco and the rebels, whereupon political liberals in America (some of them, like Senator Nye, ardent isolationists) saw the war as a struggle between democracy and fascism and urged Congress to lift the embargo on arms for the government. They ignored Soviet support of Spain's "Loyalists." Other Americans, particularly Catholics who deplored the anti-clerical ideas of the Loyalists and saw the Republic as a seedbed of communism, opposed any change of policy. As for Roosevelt, he wavered, considered a recommendation that Congress end restrictions on arms shipments to the Spanish government, but in the end decided to leave the policy unchanged. Debate over what America should do in Spain became academic early in 1939 when Franco's forces captured Barcelona and Madrid.

United States policy toward the Spanish civil war has come in for heavy criticism. In his memoirs (*On Active Service*) Henry L. Stimson, denying that the Spanish Republic had been "in any sense a purely communist government," reiterated his view of 1938 that "we should furnish arms to the government that had been recogized as legal, and to no other." Harry S. Truman, a United States senator in 1936-39, in his memoirs (*Year of Decisions*) lamented his own support of the arms embargo against "the democratic forces in Spain," adding that the embargo "was partly responsible for our losing that country as a potential ally in World War II."

Historians have taken similar positions. F. Jay Taylor in *The United States and the Spanish Civil War* (1956) says that "from the standpoint of farsighted statesmanship" Roosevelt's policy "was a blind and tragic course" which helped establish in Spain "a den of fascism which has continued to plague the body politic of Europe long after the Axis dictators were removed from the scene." In his book *The Wound in the Heart: America and the*

Spanish Civil War (1962) Allen Guttmann criticizes the American government for turning its back on liberalism in Spain, saying "it can be maintained that the abandonment of the Republic *assured* the Russian control so tirelessly exposed (often before it existed) by the Right." And William E. Leuchtenburg in *Franklin D. Roosevelt and the New Deal* chides Roosevelt for treating "the situation in Spain as though it were a local conflict of two foreign states with equal rights, not an uprising against a recognized government, and a democratic government at that." A different criticism comes from Basil Rauch (*Roosevelt: From Munich to Pearl Harbor*, 1950). In Rauch's judgment "the heaviest charge that may be laid against" administration policy is that it amounted to a concession to isolationism and hence "weakened immeasurably the effect of the President's appeals for a stronger policy against the Axis."

What determined American policy in Spain? At the time of the civil war Harold L. Ickes recorded (*The Secret Diary of Harold Ickes*, 1954) that Roosevelt told him that lifting the arms embargo for the Loyalists "would mean the loss of every Catholic voter next fall." The historian-political scientist James M. Burns (*Roosevelt: The Lion and the Fox*, 1956) accepts Ickes's estimate, saying that "Ickes had put his finger on the heart of the problem." Selig Adler in *The Uncertain Giant* is not so sure, explaining that Roosevelt's policy of an embargo on arms to both sides, "coming as it did after the Presidential election of 1936, argues against a political motive." Taylor and Guttmann in their books see noninterventionist pressure by the State Department (which Guttmann thinks came from America's habit of following the British), as well as Roosevelt's interest in the Catholic vote, as influences on the policy of neutrailty.

Roosevelt's policy in the Spanish civil war is not without defenders. The defense rests on three points: (1) contrary to the assumptions of critics (such as Truman, who says: "Republican Spain was lost on account of the embargo"), a mere lifting of the arms embargo for the Loyalists would not have changed events in Spain; (2) permitting arms to flow to Spain probably would have enlarged the conflict into a general European war, something American leaders hoped very much to avoid; (3) whatever the character of the Franco faction, it was more desirable from the standpoint of American interests than the communist-leaning Republic.

Julius Pratt in his study of Hull emphasizes the first point, stating that lifting the embargo for the Loyalists would not "have changed the outcome of the war, unless followed up by positive assistance that would in all probability have involved the United States in hostilities with Germany and Italy." In his memoirs Hull emphasizes the second point, claiming that American policy, in conjunction with that of Britain and France, succeeded in keeping the war localized. As for the third point, the argument turns on the view that, contrary to Stimson and Guttmann, the Spanish Republic in 1936 was a front for communism. Winston Churchill in *The Gathering Storm* (1948) had no doubt that the Republic had gone a long way toward communism, and indeed that "a perfect reproduction of the Kerensky period in Russia was taking place in Spain." The historian Carlton J. H. Hayes (United States ambassador to Spain during the Second World War) in *The United States and Spain* (1951) agrees with Churchill, seeing the Spanish struggle as a prelude to the post-1945 "cold war." In a similar vein Pratt concludes that a Loyalist victory would have made Spain a Soviet satellite, and "in the long pull of the cold war, better a Franco Spain than a Communist Spain."

Keeping an eye on the barbaric combat in Spain, American attention in spring 1937 again turned to neutrality, for on May 1 the Neutrailty Act of 1936 would expire. Isolationist sentiment remained strong, and it was clear that Congress would retain the arms embargo and loan prohibition. But what about trade in nonmilitary commodities? Munitions comprised only part of the needs of belligerents, and so long as American ships could carry nonmilitary cargoes to belligerent ports there still was danger of involvement in war. A total embargo, of course, would hurt the national economy, and Robert A. Divine (*The Illusion of Neutrality*) has written that Americans, "faced with the apparent choice between peace and prosperity, . . . searched for a magic formula that would preserve both." As Selig Adler (*The Uncertain Giant*) notes, "only a small minority of isolationists were willing to follow the Nye theory to its logical conclusion and embargo *all* goods to warring nations."

A solution appeared in the "cash-and-carry" idea. Bernard M. Baruch had explained it some time earlier (*Current History*, June 1936): "We will sell to any belligerent anything except lethal weapons, but the terms are 'cash on the barrel-head and come and get it.' " There was criticism that cash-and-carry would amount to benevolent neutrality in favor of wealthy countries, and Senator Hiram Johnson of California (one of a handful of isolationists who favored strict adherence to international law as the best safeguard against war) asked: "What sort of government is this and what sort of men are we to accept a formula which will enable us to sell goods and then hide?" More important were the views of the President, who offered no objection, mainly, Divine thinks, because Roosevelt "came to realize that the cash-and-carry proposal would favor Great Britain and France, with their control of the sea, if they became involved in war with Germany and Italy."

When "cash-and-carry" reached Congress a dispute arose over presidential discretion in applying the provision. Isolationists wanted its application to be mandatory; supporters of the administration wanted to let the President decide whether and under what circumstances it should be imposed. A compromise emerged. In return for sections forbidding Americans to travel on belligerent ships and prohibiting the arming of American merchantmen, isolationists accepted discretionary authority on cash-and-carry. The cash-and-carry provision would remain in force until May 1, 1939. The President could also ban shipment on American vessels of commodities which he might specify, close American ports to belligerent warships, and declare American territorial waters off-limits to belligerent submarines and merchantmen. The measure retained the arms embargo and loan prohibition of the old law and applied to civil strife as well as international war.

The new bill passed on April 29, 1937, and to prevent a lapse in neutrality it was necessary to have the presidential signature before the old law expired on May 1, which created a small problem inasmuch as Roosevelt was on a fishing cruise in the Gulf of Mexico. To beat the deadline an airplane with a copy of the bill took off from Washington on April 30. At Galveston the document was hurried aboard a navy seaplane that roared out over the Gulf and landed alongside the presidential yacht. Roosevelt signed at 6:30 A.M., on May 1.

IV

While world attention fixed on the uneasy situation in Europe, an incident in July 1937 at the Marco Polo Bridge in North China, a railway junction ten miles west of Peiping, brought matters to a crisis again in the Far East.

The Tangku truce of May 1933 ending the Manchurian affair had not weakened Japanese ambition in China, and leaders in Tokyo continued to anticipate the day when Japan would control China and extend hegemony over what they later termed "Greater East Asia." But for a time thoughts of expansion went into eclipse as Japan set out to consolidate the triumph in Manchuria. Then in 1935 Japan again turned to China, but with different tactics this time. The Japanese decided to try nonmilitary or "cold war" methods, hoping that persuasion, bribery, and intimidation would enable them to divide and conquer the loosely knit Chinese nation. The special objective of Japan's new imperialism was China's northern provinces, and through 1935-36 the Japanese sought to undermine Chiang Kai-shek's authority in North China and open the way for puppet regimes that would take orders from Tokyo.

If East Asia appeared quiet in the years after the Tangku truce, Americans remained keenly interested in what happened in that area. The historian Tang Tsou (*America's Failure in China*, 1963) credits the extensive Protestant missionary activity in China for much of this interest. He notes further that ever since the turn of the century, when Secretary Hay announced the Open Door policy, Americans had felt a curious attachment to China, seeing themselves as self-appointed guardians of that country. The Manchurian affair had heightened this benevolence toward China, and also aroused Americans against Japan. Edwin O. Reischauer in *The United States and Japan* says that "our compulsive desire to believe the worst about the Japanese pushed us towards believing only the best about the Chinese," and as a result "we gradually built up in our minds an idealized picture of China."

The government in Washington, of course, kept an eye on the Far East during the mid-1930s, and the Roosevelt administration seemed to follow the course charted by Secretary Stimson. There was no recognition of Manchukuo, and when the Japanese disregarded the Open Door in Manchuria Secretary Hull dispatched Stimson-like notes on the virtue of keeping promises. The continuity of policy was more apparent than real, however, for America's diplomacy in the Far East underwent a subtle change in those years. The idea was, instead of protest and moralizing, to build China as a counterweight to Japan, mainly by financial and technical assistance. Unfortunately the new policy failed—because of protest by Japan, the Great Depression at home, and Chiang's inability to achieve Chinese reconstruction.

It appeared by the year 1935—to American diplomatists at least—that the tide of history was running so strongly in favor of Japan that before long the Rising Sun would fly over much of China. Adjusting to reality, the United States adopted a neutral line with regard to China, and in spring 1937 Roosevelt proposed a treaty to neutralize all Pacific islands having important fortifications, a step that would have guaranteed Japanese supremacy in the western Pacific.

Then came the incident at the Marco Polo Bridge, a confusing affair in which Japanese soldiers (in the Peiping area according to the Boxer Protocol of 1901) clashed with the Chinese. The Chinese claimed that a Japanese unit on night maneuvers had demanded entry to the village of Wanping in search of a missing soldier, and when turned away had shelled the village. The Japanese charged that Chinese troops had prompted the incident by firing on them just north of the bridge.

In Washington there was hope that the incident would remain local, that commanders on the spot would work out a truce. Hope faded a few days later when Ambassador Joseph C. Grew in Tokyo reported that Japan was sending fresh troops to North China. Then came another "incident," followed on July 26 by a Japanese ultimatum that Chinese soldiers evacuate the town of Langfan. Chinese rejection of the ultimatum signaled full-scale fighting, and within weeks the Japanese were in control of the entire Peiping-Tientsin area.

Then the struggle shifted 650 miles southward to Shanghai. Fighting broke out at China's largest port early in August 1937, and in a fortnight the city was shaking under the crash of shells and bombs. The Chinese managed to hold on until November, when a Japanese flank movement compelled them to withdraw up the Yangtze toward Nanking, Chiang Kai-shek's capital. In pursuit of the retreating Chinese the Japanese unleashed air squadrons, and reports of bombs falling indiscriminately on soldiers and civilians shocked the world. At Nanking the Chinese turned to give battle, but in less than a month the Japanese sent them flying. On entering the city the Japanese, who in the past had won acclaim for their discipline and generosity toward the vanquished, reinforced a newly acquired reputation for brutality by giving themselves over to an orgy of looting and murder—the "rape of Nanking."

The "China incident," as the Japanese persisted in calling the war in China, reopened debate in America between isolationists and "interventionists." Recalling that Roosevelt had invoked the Neutrality Act in 1935 when Italy and Ethiopia went to war without formal declaration, isolationists urged him to do so again. Interventionists wanted pressure on Japan. The debate took on a new dimension when news thundered out of China about the agony of the civil population, accompanied by such headlines as "AMERICAN SCRAP IRON PLAYS GRIM ROLE IN FAR EASTERN WAR. JAPANESE RAIN DEATH WITH ONE-TIME JUNK." In the name of humanity should not the United States impose an embargo on the "sinews of war"—scrap metal, oil, cotton? But talk of an embargo raised the old question: would the Japanese retaliate?

Roosevelt and Hull concluded that the war had changed none of the premises on which earlier policy had rested. Isolationist sentiment remained intense in America, European problems prevented strong action by Britain and France, and Chiang Kai-shek's chances of beating the Japanese were nil. The best hope was that Japan might limit its ambitions in China and the Chinese might make a settlement recognizing the permanence of the Japanese presence in China. Such hope did not seem vain. Ambassador Grew in Tokyo thought there was a chance of a negotiated settlement and pleaded with his superiors in Washington to take no action that would further excite Japanese nationalism. Grew's biographer Waldo H. Heinrichs, Jr., in his splendid book *American Ambassador* (1966) writes that Grew's estimate was well-founded. Japan indeed put out "peace feelers" in October 1937, and in Heinrichs's view army leaders "still regarded the Soviet Union as the real menace and sought to avoid debilitating involvement in China." Heinrichs suspects that "increased influence in Inner Mongolia, a buffer zone in the Peking-Tientsin area, and another protecting Shanghai interests would satisfy Japan's security requirements. Elsewhere in China it was in Japan's interest for Nanking to preserve order."

Neutrality between the disputants and avoidance of action (such as an embargo on "sinews") that might arouse Japan against the United States remained the cornerstones of policy; but Roosevelt and Hull shared the national sympathy for China, and the view of Japan as a brutal aggressor. Knowing that China needed foreign arms and Japan did not, the President declined to invoke the Neutrality Act, putting off isolationists with the argument that labeling the Far Eastern affair a war would stir passions and reduce the chances of peace. Hull meanwhile had set out to rally moral pressure against Japan. His device was a highly publicized statement in July 1937 outlining American ideas about "international self-restraint," "sanctity of treaties," and "orderly processes." The statement went out to all capitals with the request that the governments express their opinions. Since (as Pratt notes) "everybody was against sin," favorable responses were soon streaming into Washington. Unfortunately the climax of Hull's maneuver coincided with the beginning of hostilities at Shanghai. Sensational news from the battle area kept reports of the general acceptance of Hull's principles off front pages, undercutting the attempt at moral suasion, and also demonstrating that the pressure of world opinion had scant influence on the Japanese.

V

The attention of diplomats next turned to Geneva, where early in October 1937 the League censured Japan as a violator of the Nine-Power and Kellogg-Briand treaties, and recommended a conference of signatories of the Nine-Power agreement and "other States which have special interests in the Far East." Secretary Hull endorsed the League action and advised officials at Geneva that the United States would take part in the conference.

Meanwhile, to mend political fences after his attempt to "pack" the Supreme Court, President Roosevelt was on a speaking tour of western states. By early October his special train was rolling eastward, and on the morning of October 5 it steamed into Chicago's Union Station. Smiling, the President left the train and prepared for the final speech of the tour. The occasion was the dedication of the new Centennial Bridge that would complete a thirty-mile system of highways along the shore of Lake Michigan. At 10:00 A.M., on a canopied platform, the President delivered the speech. Thinking perhaps of the pending parade which would portray Chicago's history, Chicagoans seemed not to grasp the meaning of Roosevelt's phrases. After the speech the President motored to the residence of George Cardinal Mundelein, had lunch, and still full of humor joined a motorcade that would take him to La Salle Street Station. He waved as throngs of people cheered and the air filled with confetti. At 2:00 P.M. he boarded his train, now on New York Central rails, and as the exhaust of the locomotive shattered the autumn calm he relaxed for the trip to Hyde Park.

Roosevelt had given one of the most memorable addresses of his presidency, the "quarantine speech." He had announced that "the peace-loving nations must make a concerted effort in opposition to those violations of treaties and those ignorings of humane instincts which today are creating a state of international anarchy and instability. . . . It seems to be unfortunately true that the epidemic of world lawlessness is spreading. When an epidemic of physical disease starts to spread, the community approves and joins in a quarantine of the patients in order to protect the health of the community against the spread of the disease. . . . War is a contagion, whether it be declared or undeclared."

It seemed that Roosevelt had made a call for hard action against the Japanese, and for many years historians accepted such an interpretation. Basil Rauch in *Roosevelt: From Munich to Pearl Harbor* (1950) saw the address as an appeal "to the American people to support collective security without limitation and as a general principle." In *The Challenge to Isolation* (1952) William L. Langer and S. Everett Gleason struck a similar note, saying that in the quarantine speech Roosevelt "broke with isolationism, discarded the policy of strict neutrality, and stepped forward as an advocate of collective security." And Robert A. Divine (*The Illusion of Neutrality*) sees the speech as marking "a radical shift in Roosevelt's outlook on world affairs."

Historians in recent years have taken a different view. Dorothy Borg in her authoritative book *The United States and the Far Eastern Crisis of 1933-1938* (1964) thinks Roosevelt never intended the speech as a signal for a new policy. Noting that he "advanced one proposal after another with bewildering rapidity" in autumn 1937, she suspects that the President was thinking out loud at Chicago, did not intend his remarks as a call for collective coercion of Japan, and had in mind only the general problem of peace across the world. William E. Leuchtenburg (*Franklin D. Roosevelt and the New Deal*) and Selig Adler (*The Uncertain Giant*) incline toward Miss Borg's interpretation.

Whatever his purpose, Roosevelt quickly drew back from the idea that the quarantine address had suggested sanctions against Japan. The day after the speech he told reporters: "Look, 'sanctions' is a terrible word to use. They are out the window." He hinted that he was thinking only of a general treaty guaranteeing "lasting peace."

Why this insistence that America was still walking softly in East Asia? Howls by isolationists and a general lack of enthusiasm for a "tough" line were partly responsible. (The President complained privately that "it's a terrible thing to look over your shoulder when you are trying to lead—and to find no one there.") The response in Tokyo also was a factor. Ambassador Grew warned that Japan's temperature was rising, and if American policy hardened there would be less chance of Japanese moderation in China.

Proof that America's policy had not changed came in the League-sponsored conference of Nine-Power Treaty signatories and "others" at Brussels in November 1937. The American delegate Norman H. Davis learned that European representatives were willing to consider sanctions against Japan. Unmoved, the State Department cabled that coercive measures did not fall within the scope of the conference—that the purpose of the Brussels meeting was to arrange a settlement between Japan and China. As discussion continued, American diplomats became nervous over newspaper stories that the United States was a leader in talk about punitive measures against Japan. Lest America be an object of Japanese wrath, as had occurred in the Manchurian affair, Secretary Hull sought adjournment of the conference. The futile deliberations came to an end on November 24, when delegates accepted a report mildly rebuking Japan as a violator of the Nine-Power Treaty.

The historian Herbert Feis (*The Road to Pearl Harbor*, 1950) has viewed the Brussels conference as a modern tragedy: "The last good chance to work out a stable settlement between China and Japan was lost in 1937." Still, it is hard to see what the conferees might have done. Isolationism and military weakness precluded coercive action by the United States. That left one option: a negotiated settlement legitimizing Japan's position in Manchuria, North China, and Shanghai. Given the temper of Americans— strong sympathy for China, hostility toward Japan—it would seem that the United States could not have acquiesced in such an arrangement. And without American concurrence any agreement would have been meaningless. Ambassador Grew probably made the best appraisal of the conference when he wrote in his diary (quoted in Borg, *op. cit.*) that the meeting never should have convened. It had been evident from the start that delegates "could never in the world agree to take *effective* measures" and would only encourage Japanese militarists by exhibiting the "lack of unity and impotence of the Powers." Grew then asked: "Why can't statesmen think things through?"

Three weeks after the debacle at Brussels the *Panay* incident occurred.

Since 1858 the United States had maintained a naval squadron on the Yangtze to protect American nationals and their interests. In December 1937 one of the gunboats, the *Panay* (named for an island in the Philippines), was trying to perform its protective mission and at the same time stay clear of both Japanese and Chinese armies as they struggled up the Yangtze. To escape Japanese artillery fire the *Panay* on December 11 left its anchorage near Nanking and steamed up the river. En route it joined three tankers belonging to the Standard-Vacuum Oil Company. Next day the four ships dropped anchor twenty-seven miles from Nanking and radioed the Japanese through the American consulate at Shanghai of their new location. The sun was shining brightly, freshly painted American flags were visible on the *Panay's* awnings, and the Stars and Stripes were flying from every mast when about 1:30 in the afternoon a squadron of twin-motored Japanese planes appeared. A *Collier's* reporter later recalled that the planes "zoomed over, reconnoitering . . . , wheeled and began lining up for the bombing." Moments later the first bomb crashed down on the gunboat, ripping a hole in the roof of the bridge. In relays the planes kept up the attack, a United Press correspondent writing that "bombs rained like hailstones and churned the waters all around the ships like geysers." When survivors tried to scramble ashore in lifeboats the Japanese planes swooped toward them, machine guns blazing. After thirty minutes the *Panay* rolled to starboard and with colors still flying sank in fifty feet of water. Three Americans were dead and forty-three injured. The tankers, also attacked, reached shore before settling to the bottom, and their crews managed to escape. Elsewhere on the Yangtze that day several British boats were targets of similar attacks.

The reaction in America was mixed. When the flag-draped coffin of one of the *Panay's* crew flashed on a New York movie screen a man jumped from his seat and commanded: "Everybody stand up!" The audience obeyed. But most people remained calm, and the *Christian Century* found hardly "the slightest trace of such frenzied excitement as followed the sinking of the *Maine* and of the *Lusitania*." Most Americans seemed to agree with Senator Borah that "it was just one of those regrettable things," or with Senator Henrik Shipstead of Minnesota that Americans should "get the hell out of China war zones."

In the State Department there was shock and outrage, and Hull sent off messages to Tokyo indicating the gravity of the attack. He soon learned that the Japanese Foreign Office was almost as upset as the State Department. To demonstrate Tokyo's good intentions the foreign minister took the unusual step of going to the American embassy to offer a "profound apology." According to the Japanese the affair had been a case of mistaken identity. Skeptics in the State Department were not convinced, but it was clear that Japan was not looking for a fight with America; the *Panay* attack had been the doing of irresponsible aviators. The Tokyo government agreed to American demands for official apologies, indemnities for the injured and relatives of the dead, assurances against future attacks, and punishment of the officers responsible for the incident.

By the end of 1937 the *Panay* affair was nearly forgotten, Japan's aggression in China was continuing, and America's Far Eastern policy had retreated to inaction.

In such manner did the world in the years 1933-37 move farther along the road to the Second World War. It is almost a truism that the United States must bear large responsibility for this tragedy; for the determination of the world's strongest country to insulate itself from Old World problems doubtless encouraged aggressors and weakened the will of peaceful countries.

Americans of the present day may decry the country's failure to meet its responsibilities thirty-odd years ago, but in the 1930s there were few who felt pangs of conscience. They saw the aggression of Japan, Italy, and Germany as a new manifestation of the Old World's habit of treaty-breaking and war, and were satisfied to be following the advice of George Washington. Reinforcing such ideas was a corps of isolationist writers who—as Warren I. Cohen shows in *The American Revisionists: The Lessons of Intervention in World War I* (1967)—were busy demonstrating that the United States had no business in the war of 1914-18, that an Allied victory had been no more preferable than a German one, and certainly not worth American involvement. If the United States had isolated itself in 1914-17 with laws akin to the neutrality measures of 1935-37, they argued, it could have avoided the war and associated calamities of debt default and depression.

The problem of staying out of war was, of course, bigger than isolationists thought, and the victory of isolation would prove transitory. Woodrow Wilson had been correct when he declared that isolation from large wars was no longer possible. As for the President and secretary of state, they saw more clearly than most, but throughout 1937 isolationists continued to restrict policy. The best the government could hope for was that in time Americans and their representatives in Congress would see the flaws in isolationist logic and liberate diplomacy from the bonds of isolationist legislation.

FOUR

Toward War in Europe

Apart from the civil war in Spain, a relative calm seemed to settle over Europe in the year 1937. Appearances were deceiving, for in Berlin the Austrian-born dictator was plotting the destruction of independent government in his own native land. He planned with the assurance of considerable support within Austria. Since the end of the World War many Austrians had been anxious to set aside the Treaty of St. Germain (1919) forbidding Austria ever to unite with Germany. They wanted their country, German in language and culture, to be part of a "greater Germany." On taking power in Berlin, Hitler encouraged such ideas, and in the mid-1930s the Austrian section of the Nazi Party became a force in Austrian affairs. For a time the Austrian government had support of Mussolini, who was nervous about Germany's territory advancing to the Brenner Pass. But by the end of 1937 Italy's dictator had reconciled himself to a German takeover in Austria. As a last resort the Austrian chancellor Kurt von Schuschnigg called for a plebiscite to let the people decide their political future. But before the Austrians could speak out, Hitler in March 1938 sent troops across the frontier, and news photographs released by the Nazis showed throngs of Austrians smiling and cheering while pretty *Fräuleins* garlanded German soldiers with flowers. After silencing opposition the Germans staged their own plebiscite, which according to Nazi accounts brought a nearly unanimous vote in favor of *Anchluss,* or union with Germany.

There was shock and dismay across Europe at this latest violation of the Paris peace settlement, but no talk of action. France had no desire for war and Britain had begun a policy of "appeasement" to head off war by "reasonable" concessions. As for the United States, Austria was a long way off and the Washington government kept its show of displeasure in bounds. It refused to recognize the *Anschluss* and suspended the commercial treaty with Austria.

Hitler had taken his boldest step to date. After parading through Vienna, the city of his tortured youth, he began to plan the next move in his grand design.

I

Hitler's object now was Czechoslovakia, and his first tactic was to stir trouble in the Sudetenland, a mountainous territory along the German-Czech border whose people were mostly German. Invoking the principle of self-determination, the dictator insisted that the Sudetenland should have the right to decide its own future, meaning the right to detach from Czechoslovakia and join the *Reich.* Loss of the Sudeten territory would deprive Czechoslovakia of its natural defensive barrier, called by Winston Churchill "the strongest fortress in Europe."

When Hitler brought the Czech dispute to the point of crisis in September 1938 the British prime minister Neville Chamberlain assumed leadership in the Anglo-French attempt to head off war and made two dramatic plane trips to Germany to urge restraint. Though Hitler was by then insisting that the Sudeten territory go to Germany without the formality of a plebiscite, he softened Chamberlain by pledging that "this is the last territorial claim I have to make in Europe," and then set a deadline for compliance with his demands. As the deadline neared he invited Chamberlain, the French premier Edouard Daladier, and Mussolini to a meeting at the Bavarian city of Munich. Conversations began at noon on September 29 and ran till two o'clock the following morning. The negotiators agreed that the Sudeten territory should pass to German control. For the Czechs the only choice seemed surrender, although Churchill *(The Gathering Storm)* later wrote that they should have stood firm, that in event of a German attack France would have honored its commitment to Czechoslovakia and Britain would have followed. Churchill thought the Allies could have beaten Germany in 1938. After the meeting Chamberlain winged back to England and before an excited crowd at the London airport on September 30 waved the declaration that Hitler had signed. As he drove through the streets of the city throngs of Britons cheered, and from a window of his residence he again waved his piece of paper, announcing: "This is the second time there has come back from Germany to Downing Street peace with honour. I believe it is peace in our time."

When the Czech problem developed in spring 1938 the United States took considerable interest, and late in May Secretary Hull issued an innocuous statement stressing America's hope for peace. When the affair neared a crisis the following August the secretary warned of "dangerous developments," and President Roosevelt in an address at Kingston, Ontario pledged support by the United States if Canadian soil were "threatened by any other empire." Rumor suggested meanwhile that Roosevelt might act as arbiter in the dispute; when that idea drew no response, the President sent messages to Hitler, Mussolini, Daladier, Chamberlain, and the Czech president Eduard Benes urging peaceful settlement. Throughout the crisis, however, Roosevelt made it plain that the United States had no intent of getting embroiled: "The Government of the

United States has no political involvements in Europe, and will assume no obligations in the conduct of present negotiations."

In the United States there was a general sigh when the crisis passed. The Munich concessions apparently did not touch American interests, had prevented war, and hopefully opened the way for better relations with Hitler. Basil Rauch (*Roosevelt: From Munich to Pearl Harbor*) has written that the President saw "the Munich Agreement meant not peace but war," but few writers are willing to credit Roosevelt with such foresight. William L. Langer and S. Everett Gleason in *The Challenge to Isolation* conclude that "Mr. Roosevelt at least momentarily shared the Prime Minister's optimism about future relations with Germany." In *Franklin D. Roosevelt and the New Deal,* William E. Leuchtenburg accepts at face value the President's confidential message to Ambassador William Phillips: "I want you to know that I am not a bit upset over the final result." And Selig Adler in *The Uncertain Giant* thinks Roosevelt shared the national sense of relief brought by the Munich arrangement, saying "the record suggests that he was willing to give appeasement one last try."

Whatever the President's estimate of the situation, such optimism as did exist inside the government was short-lived. From Paris the American ambassador William C. Bullitt reported less than a week after the Munich conference that Daladier predicted a new German demand within six months and unlike Chamberlain saw Munich as a colossal defeat. A few days later came a thunderclap from Berlin. Declaring that Germany could not rely on Chamberlain's promises, Hitler called for new German armament.

Early in 1939 the Nazi dictator prepared the destruction of Czechoslovakia. After encouraging the Slovaks to separate from the Czech Republic, Hitler alleged "disturbances" inside the country and ordered troops across the Czech frontier at 6:00 A.M., March 15. The German move came as a surprise, causing George F. Kennan, second secretary of the American legation in Prague, to report a few days later: "No one understood . . . that a trap was being prepared which was designed to bring about the end of Czechoslovakia." Pushing through howling wind and snow, German mechanized columns completed the occupation in one day. The same evening Hitler arrived in Prague and proclaimed a protectorate. Britain and France did nothing, Chamberlain explaining that disruption of the Czech state by the Slovak secession had nullified the Munich agreement. A few days later Hitler's troops entered Memel, a German city along the Baltic that had passed to Lithuanian control after the World War. The following month, on Good Friday, Mussolini sent troops across the Adriatic where they took over Albania.

The United States condemned the Axis aggression, continued to recognize the Czech and Albanian ministers, and suspended the reciprocal trade agreement with Czechoslovakia. Then the President, on April 15, 1939, made his "Saturday surprise" appeal to Hitler and Mussolini, requesting pledges that the two dictators would not attack any of thirty-one specified European and Near Eastern countries for ten years and promising American support for international conferences on trade and disarmament. From Axis capitals the appeal brought only scorn. After suggesting privately that some malady, perhaps a creeping paralysis, had inspired Roosevelt, Mussolini announced his refusal to be guided by "Messiah-like messages." In a Reichstag address that delighted Nazi auditors Hitler poured clever sarcasm on the presidential appeal. It appeared that the dictators had gotten the better of the exchange, and isolationists in America took furtive satisfaction in this foreign insolence.

The President had not expected favorable responses from the Axis capitals. In his memoirs Hull recalled that Roosevelt had intended to "put Hitler and Mussolini on the spot for what they were." The historian Julius W. Pratt (*Cordell Hull*) thinks he succeeded. A similar conclusion comes from William L. Langer and S. Everett Gleason (*The Challenge to Isolation*). In their view Roosevelt roused the American people to the imminence of danger, stigmatized the dictators as perpetrators of international discord, and heartened non-Axis countries in Europe: "The President thenceforth stood out as the moral leader in the crusade against war and thereby helped to dispel the almost universal feeling of hopelessness and despair." Charles C. Tansill is less complimentary of the President. A "revisionist" historian who thought Roosevelt in 1939-41 sought to maneuver the United States into Europe's conflict, he notes in *Back Door to War* that on the same day he appealed to them Roosevelt had publicly compared the dictators with "Huns and Vandals," and "in order to raise the pitch of their anger and make their replies so extreme in language that the American public would become increasingly war-minded, the President held a press conference on April 15 and took advantage of his gifts as a showman to impress his audience with the manner in which he had verbally spanked Hitler and Mussolini."

The President meanwhile sought revision of the neutrality law. The administration, accomplishing nothing with bills couched in verbal niceties, came out openly in May 1939 for repeal of the arms embargo. Secretary Hull carried the argument, trying to persuade congressional opinion by claiming that the embargo "conferred gratuitous benefit on the probable aggressors." The climax came in mid-July when senators of both parties gathered in the Oval Room of the White House for an evening conference with Roosevelt, Hull, and Vice-president John Nance Garner. After sandwiches and a display of the Rooseveltian charm the gentlemen got down to business. The President explained that he wanted to be able to act if war broke out in Europe; then he turned to Hull: "Cordell, what do you think about it?" While the secretary was reinforcing the presidential argument, the isolationist champion Senator Borah interrupted: "I do not believe there is going to be any war in Europe, between now and the first of January or for some time thereafter." His temper rising, Hull spoke out: "I wish the Senator from Idaho would come down to the State Department and read the dispatches which come in from all over Europe from day to day and I am sure he would change his opinion." "I don't give a damn about your dispatches," Borah roared, explaining he had private sources of information that were often more dependable than those of the State Department (according to Borah's biographer Marian C. McKenna, his sources consisted of an obscure left-wing magazine *This Week*, published in London). Tears came to Hull's eyes, and Garner finally turned to Roosevelt: "Well, Captain, we may as well face the facts. You haven't got the votes, and that's all there is to it."

Basil Rauch (*Roosevelt: From Munich to Pearl Harbor*) sees Roosevelt's defeat on the embargo issue as a victory in disguise. Isolationists, so the reasoning goes, had staked their argument on the view that war was not imminent. When the prophecy "on which the isolationists had taken their stand was so quickly proved false" the "episode was fruitful for the administration and disastrous to the isolationist cause." Other writers fail to see a silver lining. Robert A. Divine (*The Illusion of Neutrality*) views the affair as a saddening defeat for the administration and scores Roosevelt for his leadership: "Bold and precise executive leadership might have won over many wavering congressmen and stimulated a public ground swell in behalf of arms embargo repeal." As for the consequences, Hull in his memoirs wrote that he was sure the failure to lift the arms embargo had encouraged Hitler's determination to break the peace. Langer and Gleason (*The Challenge to Isolation*), on the other hand, think that by that time Nazi plans were set and repeal of the arms embargo in America would have changed nothing. Selig Adler (*The Uncertain Giant*) agrees.

The Teutonic whirlwind by now was blowing in the direction of Poland. The pretext for Hitler's latest war of nerves was the alleged inequities of the Versailles Treaty, which had carved the "Polish corridor" from German territory and made the Baltic port of Danzig an international "free city." This time the British and French resolved to stand firm, and in April 1939, they entered an an alliance with Poland to guarantee each other's territory and independence. But the decisive factor in the European equation in spring-summer 1939 was the Soviet Union. When leaders of Britain, France, and Poland hesitated to accept an alliance with the Russians, the Soviet dictator Josef Stalin turned to Hitler. Negotiations between Russia and Germany proceeded, reaching a climax on August 23, 1939 with the Non-Aggression Pact, which pledged peace and secretly agreed to a division of spoils in Eastern Europe. Following the agreement, Hitler completed preparations for an attack on Poland, and on September 1 released his torrent of fire and steel. When he refused appeals to pull back, the British and French on September 3 declared war. According to the "revisionist" writers Charles C. Tansill (*Back Door to War*) and William Henry Chamberlin (*America's Second Crusade*, 1950) the British and French honored their commitments to Poland largely because of the United States' assurances of support. In the revisionists' view the Western democracies should have held their peace. If they had,

Hitler and Stalin soon would have come to blows and the result would have been destruction of the international communist conspiracy. Tansill and Chamberlin offer flimsy evidence for the alleged assurances on the part of the United States.

It was the middle of the night in America when the storm broke, and possibly the first person in the country to be alerted was the President, roused at 3:00 A.M., by a telephone call from Ambassador Bullitt in Paris: "Mr. President, several German divisions are deep in Polish territory. . . . There are reports of bombers over the city of Warsaw." "Well, Bill," Roosevelt replied, "it has come at last. God help us all!" Within hours nearly every American knew, as millions huddled around radio receivers to hear the bulletins. Later in the day Roosevelt appealed to belligerents to renounce air attacks on civil populations. As for the country's sympathies, they were unequivocal: except for a handful of Nazi rooters and communists, Americans blamed Hitler and hoped for his defeat on the plains of Poland.

When Britain and France entered the war on September 3 the President addressed the country in a "fireside chat": "I hope the United States will keep out of this war. I believe that it will. And I give you assurance and reassurance that every effort of your Government will be directed toward that end." Unlike President Wilson in August 1914 he did not ask for impartial thinking: "I cannot ask that every American remain neutral in thought. . . . Even a neutral has a right to take account of facts. Even a neutral cannot be asked to close his mind or his conscience." Efforts were underway meanwhile to repatriate several thousand Americans caught in Europe by the outbreak; the State Department had gone on a round-the-clock schedule, setting up a system for monitoring shortwave broadcasts from Europe to speed news of military and diplomatic developments. Then on September 5 the President invoked the Neutrality Act, closing American arsenals to belligerents.

II

Even as he applied the arms embargo Roosevelt was thinking of repealing it, and when the war in Europe came to a head his plans took on new urgency. Polish armies were scattering like sheep before German tanks and clearly would be out of the war before

France and Britain could bring up forces. Whether Anglo-French arms could stop the Germans seemed questionable. Underscoring such doubt was a mid-September communication from Ambassador Joseph P. Kennedy in London that Chamberlain believed failure to gain access to American munitions "would be 'sheer disaster' for England and France."

Roosevelt composed his plans with care. His problem was to end the embargo and at the same time allay fears that this step might take the country to war. The result was a clever proposal designed to disarm isolationists while opening arsenals to the Allies. There was no mention that revision of the neutrality law would help Britain and France. The purpose was to keep America out of war. The arms embargo, according to the curious logic of the administration, threatened peace. Then, as if to becloud further the real purpose of revision, the administration struck an isolationist note. Existing law which permitted American merchantmen to enter belligerent waters with non-military cargoes, the administration contended, was inadequate to prevent the kind of "incident" most likely to involve America in war. Thus the White House proposal included provisions to shore up neutrality by prohibiting American ships from entering "danger zones" and requiring belligerents to pay cash for supplies secured in the United States and carry them away in non-American vessels. The President placed his neutrality package before a special session of Congress on September 21, 1939.

Roosevelt's charade fooled nobody. He was clearly seeking a "horse trade"—repeal of the arms embargo for provisions to keep American ships out of war zones. Isolationist members of Congress were not interested and announced that they would resist "from hell to breakfast." In the words of Senator Borah, the demand for repeal had come from the "war hounds of Europe." The next step would be extension of credit, even outright gifts, to belligerents, and after that American armies would sail to Europe. Such ideas were not in rhythm with national thinking. But Roosevelt's proposal with its blend of isolation and intervention had caught a popular mood. Americans wanted to stay out of war but also wanted to help the Allies. In response Congress on November 3, 1939, after six weeks of heated debate, passed the administration measure by large margins, and as Langer and Gleason have written, "therewith opened a new chapter in the bizarre history of American neutrality."

The revisionist school of historians, of course, has scalded Roosevelt's tactics and purpose in the neutrality debate of 1939. The most eminent revisionist, Charles A. Beard (*American Foreign Policy in the Making*), concentrates on the President's guile in emphasizing the idea that repeal of the arms embargo would strengthen neutrality. If Roosevelt was playing loosely with the truth on this point—so the revisionist inference goes—he was also not sincere when he insisted over and over that he hoped the United States would stay out of war. Selig Adler in *The Uncertain Giant* thinks the magnitude of the Nazi threat justified Roosevelt's occasional dissimulations during the neutrality debate and after: "National unity, so necessary in time of crisis, would have been further jeopardized by absolute frankness." Non-revisionist historians are otherwise unanimous in the view that the President in 1939 hoped America would avoid the European conflict.

Repeal of the arms embargo had come too late to influence events in Poland. Catching the Polish army in giant encircling maneuvers, German *Panzer* divisions had sealed Poland's fate by mid-September. To claim their share of the recent "deal" with Hitler the Soviets on September 17 invaded from the east, and eleven days later Germany and Russia agreed to a partition of Poland. Hitler then looked westward. Seeking no *lebensraum* in Western Europe, he hoped the British and French might come to terms. He hoped in vain. Confident that the Germans could not breach the French fortress system, the famous Maginot Line, the governments in Paris and London rejected the dictator's overtures. The result was a pause that extended through the winter of 1939-40, the "phony war," an appellation taken from Senator Borah's remark of October 1939 that "there is something phony about this war."

Meanwhile there erupted late in November 1939 what Julius Pratt (*Cordell Hull*) calls "a little war within the big war," the conflict between Finland and the Soviet Union precipitated by Finnish refusal to cede territory the Russians considered important to their security. Although the American people cheered the Finns, the government in Washington knew that Finland was fighting a lost cause. It also calculated that the alliance between Hitler and Stalin was shaky, and looked to the day when the Russians, as Hull later recalled, "would come over to the side of the Allies." The object of policy, then, was to avoid a break with Russia. The "Winter War" ended in March 1940. Finland retained its independence but lost part of its territory and had to make military and economic concessions.

A month later Europe again heard the rumble of Hitler's war mechanism, a signal that the "phony war" was over. In lightning —*blitz*—maneuvers the Germans in April 1940 occupied Denmark and Norway. Next they turned southward to the Netherlands, Belgium, Luxembourg, and the main prize, France. When Hitler launched his French offensive in May 1940 it appeared that he was following the same route as the Kaiser's armies in 1914. Then, while everyone focused on the German "right wing," the dictator sent his main force crashing though the Ardennes Forest. Within a fortnight German arms had shattered French defenses and were sweeping behind the Maginot Line toward Paris. Hitler was about to accomplish in a few weeks what the Kaiser had been unable to do in four years of the First World War. The only event of some reassurance in those terrible spring weeks was evacuation in late May of 300,000 British soldiers from the beaches of Dunkirk.

As Allied armies fell back, the French premier Paul Reynaud appealed to America for a declaration of war on Germany. In the view of the revisionist writer Charles C. Tansill (*Back Door to War*) Roosevelt had already committed the United States to take part in the war in Europe, but could not act at this time: "His campaign for re-election as President would soon take shape and he knew he could not hope for success if the voters knew that he was secretly putting America into World War II." Tansill's theory is without proof. Most historians agree with Julius Pratt (*Cordell Hull*) that the United States simply "had little that it could immediately contribute other than its productive capacity, and this was already at the disposal of the Allies." The most the United States could do was to urge Italy to stay out of the war. Mussolini's reply was an attack on France in the south, provoking Roosevelt's famous utterance that "on this tenth day of June 1940, the hand that held the dagger has struck it into the back of its neighbor." All was over when French leaders surrendered on June 22, in the same railway carriage in which Germans had signed the armistice of November 11, 1918.

Unlike many Americans, Roosevelt was not ready to consider the British defeated and had decided several weeks before the collapse of France to see Britain through the crisis. He directed the State Department to seek legal ways of supplying Britain with guns, ammunition, and planes from stock belonging to the United States government. Under the recent neutrality law, of course, it was lawful to sell armaments to belligerents; but their sale by a neutral government was close to a patent violation of international law. Private agents in a neutral country could sell munitions to a belligerent; the government could not. The solution was to sell government-owned armaments to private interests for resale to the British. After making sure that Congress had no major objection, Roosevelt threw open the government's arsenals, and within weeks guns and planes began to arrive in Atlantic ports for shipment to Britain. He advised the country of his intentions in a speech at Charlottesville, Virginia on June 10, 1940, saying that "we will extend to the opponents of force the material resources of this nation." With those words, according to Julius Pratt (*Cordell Hull*), "the President unequivocally abandoned any pretense of old-fashioned neutrality toward the wars in Europe and Asia. Increasingly from now on the position of the United States was that of a nonbelligerent."

At the same time, in June 1940, Roosevelt sought to give his foreign policy a bipartisan flavor by bringing two prominent Republicans into his cabinet, Henry L. Stimson as secretary of war and Frank Knox as secretary of the navy. Stimson and Knox were in full accord with the President's ideas about the war, and Basil Rauch (*Roosevelt: From Munich to Pearl Harbor*) thinks "the ability of Americans, led by Roosevelt, Stimson and Knox, to transcend their domestic quarrels and political predilections in the face of foreign danger once more rescued the Republic from diseases which had helped kill such a great nation as France." The revisionist Charles C. Tansill (*Back Door to War*) takes a less exalted view. Calling Stimson "a notorious war hawk," he writes: "It is apparent that after June 1940 the Administration embarked upon a phony bipartisan policy that pointed directly to American intervention in the European conflict."

While the program of supplying Britain was getting under way, the United States in summer 1940 faced the question of whether to establish diplomatic relations with the new French government, the so-called Vichy regime, in the part of France that Hitler had chosen not to occupy. The argument against dealing with Vichy turned on the fact that the regime was authoritarian and many of its leaders were Nazi collaborators. On the other hand establishment of diplomatic relations would give the United States a peephole for observing Hitler's flank. There also was the chance that American representatives at Vichy could minimize Nazi influence, keep Vichy from declaring war on Britain, and prevent remaining French naval and colonial assets from passing to Hitler.

After much soul-searching the Roosevelt administration decided to establish relations with the Vichy government, and the historian William L. Langer (*Our Vichy Gamble,* 1947) writes that "the so-called Vichy policy drew more criticism of the Department of State than almost any other issue of foreign affairs during the war years." Still, Langer defends the policy: "From the standpoint of American interests, the policy was always a substantially sound one even though it may have been an unattractive one." He then reminds the reader that the argument against dealing with Vichy rested on sentiment or ideology. "Such considerations," he says, "are dangerous if they are made the basis for foreign policy." Louis Gottschalk ("Our Vichy Fumble," *Journal of Modern History*, XX, 1948) scores Langer for dismissing ideological considerations as unimportant in framing foreign policy and suggests that had the United States renounced "opportunism" and put its weight behind "a genuinely anti-Fascist, democratic war" the result might have been a speedier victory and a more stable peace.

III

In Europe meanwhile Hitler was meeting frustration. Relations with the Soviet Union had become troubled, causing the Nazis to fear for their eastern flank, and the British were giving no sign that they accepted defeat. "Operation Sea Lion," the invasion of the British Isles, had run into delay, chiefly because the Royal Air Force was denying the Germans mastery of English skies. To take care of the R.A.F., the Germans in August 1940 launched a massive air campaign to destroy British airfields and planes. Discouraged by losses, the Germans after a few weeks changed tactics and turned their bombing planes on Britain's cities, hoping to bring the country to terms by terrorizing the civil population. Night after night through autumn 1940 warning sirens howled, people scurried to shelters, searchlights pierced the darkness. Then came the din of airplane motors, anti-aircraft guns, and exploding bombs. When the bombers left there was the task of putting out fires and digging through the rubble for victims. But the morale of Britain's people refused to crack.

When the "Battle of Britain" began President Roosevelt was wrestling with a request by Britain's new prime minister, Winston Churchill (he had taken office in May 1940), that the United States transfer part of its destroyer fleet to the Royal Navy. The British had barely 100 destroyers to escort convoys across the Atlantic and guard against a German invasion; the United States had 240 destroyers in commission and another 57 under construction. Roosevelt wanted to answer Churchill's appeal, but several questions appeared. In view of America's defense needs, were the ships expendable? What would happen to the vessels if Hitler managed to defeat Britain? Was there legal basis for a transfer? Would it provoke the isolationists? A presidential election was only a few months away; what would be the political consequences? Would transfer of destroyers produce a German declaration of war against the United States?

One by one the questions received answers. Military chiefs reported that the country could spare fifty destroyers, and the British pledged that in the "impossible contingency" of Germany overrunning the British Isles the ships would not go to Hitler. There were assurances that any transaction would be legal, and as for the isolationists, supporters of Britain noted that the London and Washington governments had already discussed American bases on British territory in the Western Hemisphere. Why not exchange the destroyers for bases? Isolationists for years had demanded such bases as a price for canceling the "war debts" of 1917-19. As for the election, Roosevelt, communicating through the distinguished newspaper editor William Allen White, a Republican, sought to offset the effect of a destroyer transfer by urging the Republican presidential candidate Wendell L. Willkie to announce support. Willkie agreed to keep a destroyer-bases transaction out of the campaign but declined to declare his support of it, whereupon Roosevelt concluded that what was good for the country was good politics. Would Germany declare war? Roosevelt was confident that Hitler would tolerate a great deal to avoid a clash with the country that had shattered German dreams in 1917-18.

Pressing on with negotiations, Roosevelt faced a final problem. Should he seek consent of Congress? Failure to do so would offend congressional sensibilities and bring charges of dictatorial action. But a congressional debate would give isolationists a forum and might lead to repudiation of a destroyer transfer. In any event a debate would be long-drawn-out and the British could ill afford to wait for the ships. The President decided to arrange for the transfer by executive order.

Negotiations ended on September 2, 1940 when Secretary Hull and the British ambassador signed papers for the transfer of fifty destroyers of First World War vintage. At the same time the British leased locations for American bases in Newfoundland, Bermuda, the Bahamas, Jamaica, St. Lucia, Antigua, Trinidad, and British Guiana. Next day Admiral Harold R. Stark certified that possession of the bases rendered the destroyers unimportant to America's defense, whereupon the ships, described by Churchill as "more precious than rubies," steamed out of United States ports. Viewing the trade of fifty old "four-stackers" for a string of bases as a sharp bargain, most Americans applauded. The largest criticism was that Roosevelt had acted high-handedly in failing to clear the transaction with Congress, Willkie assailing the transfer by executive order as "the most dictatorial action ever taken by any President."

What were the consequences of the destroyer deal? Sumner Welles (*The Time for Decision,* 1944) wrote that "had the British Navy not been enabled at once to use the fifty American destroyers for escort protection, England might well have been beaten down before the winter months had gone by." Britons have taken a more restrained view of the value of the ships. Philip Goodhart (*Fifty*

Ships that Saved the World, 1965) quotes one British admiral as saying: "I thought they were the worst destroyers I had ever seen, poor seaboats with appalling armament and accommodation. The price paid for them was scandalous." Another admiral said: "A contemporary naval opinion . . . would be that although the U.S. vessels were tactically of the lowest order, and unsuited to the Atlantic weather, their mere presence threshing about in the water around the convoy afforded some sort of deterrent against the U-boat. . . ."

More important were the diplomatic results. The deal was an abandonment of any pretense of neutrality. It was an act of war, for there was no subtle deference to international law by selling the ships first to private agents. In the words of Langer and Gleason (*The Challenge to Isolation*): "The country had come to recognize its stake in the survival and ultimate victory of Britain, and it could already be predicted with considerable confidence that in the future American policy would proceed, though reluctantly and regretfully, to any lengths required for the defeat of Hitler and his allies." Seeing America's abandonment of neutrality as one of the crucial developments in the war, Goodhart, a British writer, concludes that "before they had fired a shot or dropped a depth charge these fifty ships made a unique contribution to the salvation of the western world." Fortunately Hitler in 1940 was not spoiling for a fight with America. According to Hans L. Trefousse (*Germany and American Neutrality*, 1951), "conflict with the United States prior to complete victory in Europe was . . . the last thing Hitler wanted and he did not declare war."

Revisionist writers, of course, score the destroyer deal. William Henry Chamberlin (*America's Second Crusade*) calls it "a new milestone on America's road to war." Like Tansill (*Back Door to War*), Chamberlin also castigates the exchange as illegal. Although he agrees that the legal basis of the transaction was weak, Donald F. Drummond (*The Passing of American Neutrality*, 1955) speaks for non-revisionists when he asserts that "the main issue was the value of the exchange in terms of national defense; and considered retrospectively, its wisdom can hardly be doubted."

If the destroyer deal marked an open abandonment of neutrality, it did not weaken America's desire to stay out of war. Proof of this came in the closing days of the election campaign of 1940.

It seemed that foreign policy would not be a campaign issue in 1940. During their national conventions both Democrats and Republicans had adopted platform resolutions on the subject that were almost identical, and the presidential candidates, Willkie and Roosevelt, hardly differed in their ideas on foreign affairs. Then, late in October, opinion polls showed Roosevelt running in front, at which point Republican leaders persuaded Willkie to forget bipartisanship and assail the President as an interventionist who would take the country to war. Contemptible as such charges were (Willkie later confessed that "in moments of oratory in campaigns we all expand a little bit"), it was clear that the G.O.P. candidate had struck a responsive chord.

Roosevelt countered with equally deplorable tactics, identifying Willkie with such Republican isolationists as Representatives Joseph W. Martin, Jr., Hamilton Fish, and Bruce Barton. Playful repetition of the catchy phrase "Martin, Barton, and Fish" brought roars of laughter from Democratic audiences, but Robert E. Sherwood (*Roosevelt and Hopkins,* 1948) observed that it did little to reassure anxious mothers and fathers. So Roosevelt declared in a speech at Boston: "I have said this before, but I shall say it again and again: Your boys are not going to be sent into any foreign wars." When advisers suggested adding the words "except in case of attack" the President had replied that "if somebody attacks us, then it isn't a foreign war." The statement served the immediate purpose, and Roosevelt won the election. Later, after he led the country into war following Japan's attack on Pearl Harbor, political enemies resurrected the pledge and, ignoring subtleties about "foreign wars," used it against him. Believing that he had already determined to involve the country in Europe's war, revisionist historians see the Boston speech as further proof of Roosevelt's duplicity: Tansill, for instance, saying that "the American people . . . had to be fooled by pacific phrases."

IV

Despite Hitler's inability to mount an invasion of Britain, the Axis star in summer and early autumn of 1940 continued to rise. Awed by the conquest of France, Hungary joined forces with Hitler in July. To the east of Hungary was Rumania, in the shadow of the Reich and the Soviet Union. Independent Rumania expired peaceably in October, cut up by the Soviets and Nazis. Mussolini in mid-September had carried the war to North Africa, moving Italian divisions against the British in Egypt, and two weeks later the alliance added a new partner, Japan, whose representatives met in Berlin with leaders of Germany and Italy and put their hands to the Tripartite Pact.

Then the alliance began to lose some of its luster. In October, Mussolini sent armies into Greece. The Greeks counterattacked and within a month the Italians were reeling. In North Africa the Italians invasion of Egypt ran out of steam, and a British counterstroke in December 1940 sent the Italians flying back into Libya. Hitler also was having trouble. Spain continued to resist alliance with the Axis and, more serious, Britain refused to collapse under merciless air attack. When it became clear that his bombers were not winning the Battle of Britain, Hitler at the end of 1940 turned his attention to England's oceanic lifeline, hoping that U-boats might starve the British into submission.

German submarines were only a part of the threat to Britain's survival as 1941 drew near; equally serious, British dollar reserves were running low, threatening Britain's capacity to purchase supplies in the United States. When this problem had arisen in the First World War help had come from American bankers and, after April 1917, from the American government. This time, however, there were legal barriers to such transactions—the neutrality law's ban on loans to belligerents and the Johnson Act's prohibition of loans to countries that had defaulted First World War debts to the American government.

While on a Caribbean cruise in December 1940 President Roosevelt received an urgent communication from Churchill spelling out Britain's plight. On returning to the capital he sought a way to meet the problem, and in the end divined a solution in what Secretary of the Treasury Henry Morgenthau, Jr., described as one of his "brilliant flashes." Recalling that the United States had arranged to lend cargo vessels to Britain with the stipulation that they be returned after the war, the President asked: why not extend "lend-lease" to guns, tanks, and planes?

To outline his plan, Roosevelt, tanned and jaunty, on December 17, 1940 held one of his most memorable press conferences. Furtively disclaiming "any particular news," he opened the session by announcing that Britain's survival was important to the defense of America. He ridiculed as "nonsense" the traditional methods of financing war and proposed that the United States lend armaments to Britain. Then came the parable of the garden hose: "Suppose my neighbor's home catches fire, and I have a length of garden hose four or five hundred feet away. If he can take my garden hose and connect it up with his hydrant, I may help him to put out the fire. Now what do I do? I don't say to him before that operation, 'Neighbor, my garden hose cost me fifteen dollars; you have to pay me fifteen dollars for it.' No! What is the transaction that goes on? I don't want fifteen dollars— I want my garden hose after the fire is over." With that homely analogy, Robert E. Sherwood later wrote (*Roosevelt and Hopkins*), "Roosevelt won the fight for Lend Lease." The victory was not immediately apparent, and to rouse support the President went before a national radio audience on December 29 and delivered the "arsenal of democracy" speech. He declared that the best way to defend the Western Hemisphere was to help Britain, denied that lend-lease would push the United States toward war ("you can . . . nail any talk about sending armies to Europe as a deliberate untruth"), and explained that "we must be the great arsenal of democracy."

The bill to establish lend-lease—H.R. 1776—went before Congress on January 10, 1941. The origin of the interesting legislative number is obscure, although Sherwood wrote that "it sounds like a Rooseveltian conception, for it was the veritable declaration of interdependence." (The revisionist Charles Tansill in *Back Door to War* takes a less exalted view, writing that in the year 1776 "we declared our independence from Britain; in 1941 we put it into grave peril by giving Britain a blank check which Churchill filled in with great gusto and then sent back to Washington for Roosevelt's indorsement [sic].") Isolationists responded sourly, Senator Robert A. Taft of Ohio observing that "lending war equipment is a good deal like lending chewing gum. You don't want it back." Senator Burton K. Wheeler of Montana compared lend-lease with the Agricultural Adjustment Administration's cotton "plow-up" of 1933, calling it "the New Deal's triple-A foreign policy; it will plough under every fourth American boy." Wheeler's remark brought the only presidential retort in the lend-lease debate: Roosevelt called the attack "the rottenest thing that has been said in public life in my generation," adding: "Quote me on that."

Congressional debate over H.R. 1776 was sharp, but the measure clearly had the necessary votes. In the House the bill carried 317-71, proof of the great national support for lend-lease. The President signed the measure on March 11, 1941. From Britain, Churchill hailed the legislation as a "new Magna Carta," declaring that "the words and acts of the President and people of the United States come to us like a draught of life, and they tell us by an ocean-borne trumpet call that we are no longer alone."

Noting the large bipartisan support for H.R. 1776, Basil Rauch (*Roosevelt: From Munich to Pearl Harbor*) calls the lend-lease debate "a remarkable display of democracy in action" and sees the resulting act as "a great, practical effort to oppose aggression and support its victims." Revisionist writers, as one would expect, have taken a different line. In their view the legislation was another part in Roosevelt's design to maneuver the United States into war. Charles Tansill (*Back Door to War*) calls H.R. 1776 the "back door to intervention in World War II," while Charles A. Beard (*President Roosevelt and the Coming of the War,* 1948), considering the legislation an act of war, sees cynicism in the administration's insistence that it was a measure for defense and peace. William Henry Chamberlin (*America's Second Crusade*) calls the legislation confusing, but "confusion of public opinion was what Roosevelt needed gradually to steer America into undeclared hostilities while professing devotion to peace."

One need not accept the conspiracy ideas of the revisionists to acknowledge that lend-lease took the country to the very edge of the European conflict. Having gambled its wealth on Britain's survival, the United States was not apt to stand by and watch its investment go down if an Axis victory appeared imminent. Selig Adler, generally sympathetic with Roosevelt's policy, says (*The Uncertain Giant*), "the noninterventionists had correctly predicted that the adoption of lend-lease would mark a point of no return for the United States," and Julius Pratt *(Cordell Hull)* says that when the President signed H.R. 1776 "the United States entered fully into the condition of nonbelligerency."

One should note here a non-revisionist criticism of Roosevelt's policy in early 1941; he should not have waited for the Axis to strike, but should have moved to put America's armed strength in the balance. The best expression of this view came in the postwar memoirs of Secretary Stimson *(On Active Service)*. Stimson cites a Gallup Poll of April 1941 finding that three-fourths of the people favored entering the war "if it appeared certain that there was no other way to defeat Germany and Italy." According to Stimson, "the most striking fact about this result was that in the considered view of the leaders of the American Government, and also by facts publicly known, it was already clear that 'there was no other way to defeat Germany and Italy' than by American entry into the war." As Stimson saw it, the President should have put together those pieces of intelligence—the poll and expert opinion on Britain's chances—and begun to condition Americans for belligerency. Instead Roosevelt "in effect surrendered the initiative to the Nazis" and "left it to them to choose their time to fight."

Hitler by spring 1941 had turned to the south and east. Across the Mediterranean a new commander, Erwin Rommel, had opened up the theater in North Africa, and in a series of spectacular maneuvers in April sent the British reeling toward the Egyptian border. That same month Hitler sent armies crashing into the Balkans. Resistance there was fierce, but in less than three weeks the Nazi banner fluttered over Yugoslavia and Greece. Then the dictator wheeled his forces around and in June 1941 astonished the world by launching "Operation Barbarossa," the invasion of the Soviet Union.

Germany's move into Russia touched off an angry debate in the United States. Should lend-lease assistance go to the Soviets, leaders of world communism, parties to Hitler's crime against Poland, the rapists of Finland? Agreeing with Senator Bennett

Champ Clark that "Stalin is as bloody-handed as Hitler," many Americans wanted to stand apart from the Nazi-Soviet war. Others endorsed the idea of Missouri's junior senator, Harry S. Truman: "If we see that Germany is winning we ought to help Russia and if Russia is winning we ought to help Germany." Not everyone agreed. *The New York Times* saw a German victory in Russia as the key to Nazi domination of the world, and when German divisions smashed forward on all fronts such argument became more persuasive. After Congress overwhelmingly rejected an amendment to a lend-lease appropriation bill prohibiting aid to Russia, the President, in November 1941, declared the Soviet Union eligible for lend-lease assistance.

With Hitler distracted in Russia, Roosevelt in mid-summer 1941 decided the time opportune for a meeting with Churchill. An informal exchange of views might open the way for even closer cooperation. Churchill was agreeable, and secret arrangements went forward for a shipboard rendezvous off the coast of Newfoundland near Argentia. On August 3, Roosevelt, supposedly on a fishing cruise, went aboard the yacht *Potomac* at New London, but at sea transferred to the cruiser *Augusta* for the trip to Argentia. Churchill crossed the choppy North Atlantic on the new battleship *Prince of Wales.*

The Argentia discussions focused on the problems of beating Germany and heading off Japan, but posterity has been more intrigued with an almost incidental by-product of the conference: the famous Atlantic Charter, a joint declaration of Anglo-American war aims. Similar to the Fourteen Points proposed by Woodrow Wilson in 1918, the charter announced that the United States and Britain sought no new territory, favored self-determination for all people and an equitable distribution of the world's wealth, determined to destroy nazism, and advocated an international organization which after the war would guarantee such blessings of peace as freedom of seas and disarmament.

What was the object of the charter? For Churchill it identified the United States and Britain more closely and brought the Americans a step nearer the war. Roosevelt thought more widely. Despite the joking informality of the Atlantic Conference he did not fully trust the British, and saw the joint declaration as a device to head off secret agreements of the type that brought so much trouble after the First World War. Hopefully it would also rally people in occupied countries to defy the Nazis, and by pledging an equitable peace might even move Germans to oppose Hitler. It would clothe the war in the guise of a crusade, and the experience of 1917-18 notwithstanding, Americans loved crusades. Then too, a charter ringing with exalted phrases would obscure the main business at Argentia, the discussion of war plans, and spike isolationist criticism of the meeting.

V

If, as Roosevelt assured the country, the conference at Argentia did not take the United States along the road to war, events elsewhere around the Atlantic were doing just that.

At the beginning of 1941, as mentioned, Hitler put increased emphasis on the war at sea, and while lend-lease was under consideration in America the "Battle of the Atlantic" was expanding, raising the question of how the United States and Britain could make sure that merchant vessels carrying lend-lease cargoes would get past German submarines and cruisers and find their way safely to British ports. There seemed only one answer, convoys. But convoys required escort and the Royal Navy could not spare the necessary destroyers and cruisers. American warships were a requisite. Lest it wreck lend-lease, American interventionists tried to pass over the convoy issue before enactment of H.R. 1776. At a news conference Roosevelt shrugged off the question of convoy escort as a mere detail, and ultimately the administration accepted an amendment to H.R. 1776 that "nothing in this Act shall be construed to authorize or to permit the authorization of convoying by naval vessels of the United States."

Still, it seemed idiotic to stand by and watch U-boats destroy lend-lease cargoes; some individuals playfully suggested that it would be simpler to dump supplies into the Atlantic from American piers. Convoy escort by American naval vessels in truth was inevitable. Donald F. Drummond (*The Passing of American Neutrality*) writes that "with the adoption of Lend-Lease it would no longer be a question of whether the United States Navy should be used for convoy duty, but rather a question of when such action might become absolutely necessary." Everyone knew the consequences of such a step. As Selig Adler explains *(The Uncertain Giant)*, "convoying would lead to an undeclared naval war with Germany."

Fearing the isolationists, Roosevelt still turned aside appeals that he order the Atlantic fleet to escort lend-lease convoys. Then in April 1941 he set up a "neutrality patrol" by American ships and planes in the western Atlantic. The mission of the patrol was to "observe and report" belligerent movements and keep war from "our front doors." By flashing locations of German U-boats, of course, the patrol would alert merchantmen to veer away and invite British cruisers and destroyers to attack. Since American ships and planes had no authority to attack, Roosevelt insisted that the operation was indeed a patrol, not an escort. He explained that there was the same difference between a patrol and an escort as between a cow and a horse, and "if one looks at a cow and calls it a horse that is all right with the President, but that does not make a cow a horse."

To broaden the neutrality patrol Roosevelt signed an agreement in April 1941 with the Danish government that brought Greenland into "our sphere of co-operative hemispheric defense." Next he turned to Iceland. Although British and Canadian troops had occupied Iceland for a year, the President nevertheless feared a German takeover, and even more so when a clash between the American destroyer *Niblack* and a German U-boat (the first combat for the United States of the war) indicated new German activity in the area. Encouraged by the British, Iceland accepted American "protection," and a brigade of Marines arrived at the island early in July 1941.

The presence of American forces required convoys to operate between the United States and Iceland, raising the question: why not permit British lend-lease ships to join convoys for protection as far as Iceland? Roosevelt wavered, then drew back, but under British pressure at the Atlantic conference he gave in, pledging that he would authorize convoys bound for Iceland to take in British ships. In the view of the revisionist writer Harry Elmer Barnes *(Perpetual War for Perpetual Peace,* 1953)the decision to protect convoys was "a thinly veiled effort to lure Germany into a much desired act of war." Convoy escort by the American navy began in late August, but the President, fearing the public reaction, declined to issue official orders.

How did Hitler respond to America's interference in the war at sea? Concentrating on the eastern campaign, he rejected his navy's appeals for authority to attack American ships, and when a U-boat operating in the south Atlantic in May 1941 sank the merchantman *Robin Moor* (the first American ship to go down) he reiterated his wish that Germany "avoid any incident with the U.S.A." As Hans L. Trefousse *(Germany and American Neutrality)* emphasizes, the dictator would not be diverted from his plan of dealing with enemies one at a time. Until he finished with the Soviets he did not wish to face the Americans. His object in 1940-41 was to divert American attention to the Pacific by encouraging the Japanese, which according to Trefousse was his main purpose in bringing Japan into the Axis alliance.

Incidents were inevitable, and on September 4, 1941 the American destroyer *Greer* and the *U-652* exchanged shots in waters two hundred miles southwest of Iceland. En route to Reykjavik with mail and passengers, the *Greer,* an old "four-stacker" dating from 1918, received a message from a British patrol plane that a submarine was lying submerged ten miles ahead. Alarm gongs sounded "general quarters" and the *Greer* set out after the U-boat. With sounding devices it made contact, while a message giving the submarine's location brought a British plane that dropped four depth charges. The submarine fired a torpedo, the *Greer* dodged, and the torpedo crossed a hundred yards astern. The *Greer's* answer was a pattern of eight depth charges. A few minutes later the submarine fired another torpedo that also missed. The *Greer* dropped a few more depth charges, then proceeded to Iceland.

Roosevelt determined to make the most of the *Greer* affair. Although he had already quietly authorized the Atlantic fleet to escort lend-lease convoys as far as Iceland, he fretted over how to break the news to the country. In the *Greer* episode he saw his opportunity. He would present the decision to escort as a response to a German outrage. Portrayed as Nazi aggression, the incident also opened the way for orders removing restrictions on the neutrality patrol. He would direct the fleet to "shoot on sight" at

Axis submarines and cruisers operating in America's "defensive waters" (the entire Atlantic west of Iceland).

Delayed several days because of the death of his mother Sara Delano Roosevelt, the President on September 11 prepared for a radio address. That evening, a mourning band on his sleeve, he entered the diplomatic reception room of the White House. Underscoring the historical importance were portraits of past Presidents, a bust of Lafayette, and the large clock from the San Francisco Exposition of 1906. Sitting around the room were Mrs. Roosevelt, members of the family, friends, aides, photographers. The President moved to a cluttered desk and sat down before a small microphone. Not mentioning that the *Greer* had provoked the U-boat, he said in solemn tones that the destroyer "was carrying mail to Iceland. . . . She was then and there attacked by a submarine. . . . I tell you the blunt fact that the German submarine fired first upon this American destroyer without warning, and with deliberate design to sink her." He emphasized "the Nazi danger to our Western World," then declared that "when you see a rattlesnake poised to strike, you do not wait until he has struck before you crush him." Calling German submarines "the rattlesnakes of the Atlantic," he announced that American ships and planes "will no longer wait until Axis submarines lurking under water, or Axis raiders on the surface of the sea, strike their deadly blow—first." They would shoot on sight. Then the President discussed convoy escort. Explaining that the fleet had the duty of "maintaining the American policy of freedom of the seas," he announced that patrolling vessels and planes "will protect all merchant ships—not only American ships but ships of any flag—engaged in commerce in our defensive waters." When the President finished, one of the broadcasting networks played *The Star-Spangled Banner*. Roosevelt and the others in the room stood at attention.

The President had made no false statements, but by omitting to mention that the destroyer had provoked the submarine he presented a distorted view of the *Greer* incident. To revisionist writers this was just another of Roosevelt's cynical maneuvers to get the United States in the war. In the words of William Henry Chamberlin (*America's Second Crusade*), "Bismarck's editing of the Ems telegram was a masterpiece of straightforwardness compared with

Roosevelt's picture of the *Greer* as a peaceful mail-carrier, wantonly set on by a hostile submarine." Even Langer and Gleason (*The Undeclared War*, 1953), though sympathetic with most of Roosevelt's policies, find it hard to defend this speech. They suggest that perhaps Roosevelt's remarks rested on the best information available at the time of the speech, then add: "This does not, however, exonerate the President of the charge of having exploited the incident without awaiting a detailed report."

The President in the weeks that followed urged repeal of "crippling provisions" contained in the neutrality law. His main target was articles prohibiting the arming of American merchantmen and preventing American ships from entering "danger zones." He declared that he was asking Congress to carry out the intent of the Lend-Lease Act: "In other words, I ask for Congressional action to implement Congressional policy. Let us be consistent." Their spirit unimpaired, isolationists rallied together against the presidential request. Then came news on October 17 that German torpedoes had ripped the destroyer *Kearny,* killing eleven men. The *Kearny* had projected itself into a battle between Allied warships and German submarines near Iceland, but details were obscure and the affair moved the House of Representatives to vote away the prohibition on arming merchant ships.

Next came Roosevelt's sensational "Navy Day" speech on October 27 in which he announced that the *Kearny* was not just a navy ship: "She belongs to every man, woman and child in the nation." He also revived memories of the Zimmermann Telegram of 1917, announcing that he had received a secret Nazi map that divided South America into "five vassal states" and referred to a Nazi plan to "abolish all existing religions." Then came a new disaster. On October 31 the destroyer *Reuben James* fell victim of a German submarine while escorting a convoy near Iceland, taking down more than a hundred seamen. The following week debate in Congress over revision of the neutrality law reached a climax, and in an atmosphere heavy with tension the Senate on November 7 voted 50-37 for repeal of the remaining restrictions. Six days later, by a vote of 212-194, the lower chamber did likewise.

The United States had declared naval war on Germany and full-scale war could not be far behind, for as Senator Wheeler said:

"You cannot shoot your way a little bit into war any more than you can go a little bit over Niagara Falls."

Langer and Gleason *(The Undeclared War)* have written that the historian's appraisal of America's policy toward the European war down to December 1941 "will depend on whether or not he agrees with Mr. Roosevelt's conclusion that Hitlerism constituted a menace to the United States and to the principles on which the nation was founded, and that therefore it was in the national interest to support the opponents of Nazism and contribute to Hitler's defeat." Accepting the view that Hitler was such a menace, the two authors approve the general outline of American policy. More recent support for the view that Hitler threatened interests of the United States has come from the historians Alton Frye and James V. Compton. In his book *Nazi Germany and the American Hemisphere, 1931-1941* (1967) Frye has documented Hitler's hostility to the United States, his plans for enlarging German influence in South America, and Nazi subversive activity throughout the Western Hemisphere. Referring to the Berlin government's readiness to intervene in the politics of American nations, he concludes that "this tendency in itself posed an insidious and potentially vital threat to the stability and character of American political institutions" and adds that "it is certainly reasonable to conclude that such intervention could have grown worse if the New Order had become firmly established in Europe." Compton takes a similar approach in *The Swastika and the Eagle: Hitler, the United States, and the Origins of World War II* (1967). Conceding the absence of any Nazi plans for the military conquest of the Western Hemisphere, Compton nonetheless believes that "inflated by success and drawn along by a certain momentum of conquest, Hitler [had he beaten Britain and Russia] would not have indefinitely confined himself to Europe." Even if the German leader had wanted to limit his empire to the area between the British Isles and the Urals, Compton thinks "the economic and political effects of his conquests on America to say nothing of the ideological tension would have virtually nullified any hope of avoiding a collision between the United States and a Nazi Europe." Ergo, Roosevelt, in terms of

American interests, took the proper course when he abandoned neutrality and arrayed the United States against Germany.

In accord with the view that the United States in 1939-41 had ample reason to oppose Hitler, Hans L. Trefousse *(Germany and American Neutrality)* makes an even higher estimate of Roosevelt's policies. Where Langer and Gleason and other historians see Roosevelt as cautiously backing and filling in response to Hitler's successes and Allied needs, Trefousse presents the President as one who skillfully out-maneuvered the dictator. He explains that Hitler's pattern in Europe had been to exploit the peaceful hopes of intended victims: "The victims, hoping against hope that they might be spared, refused to abandon their neutrality until it was too late, thus playing directly into their adversary's hands." Such had been the intent of Hitler's American policy. He sought to neutralize the United States until he had achieved victory in Europe, whereupon "an isolated America would have to face an overbearing Germany single-handed." Hitler's policy failed. "Under the leadership of Franklin D. Roosevelt, America refused to be caught unaware and took the liberty of defending herself, building up her own armed establishment and rendering all possible aid to the Allies." Trefousse concludes that "this line of action was Mr. Roosevelt's great contribution to American foreign policy."

There are dissenters, historians—the so-called revisionists—who accept the ideas of prewar isolationists that Hitler was not a threat to the Western Hemisphere and hence the United States should have insulated itself from the European conflict. The most prominent exponents of such views have been Charles A. Beard and Charles C. Tansill. If one agrees that the war in Europe did not concern the United States, the Beard-Tansill case against Roosevelt's European policies in 1939-41 is strong.[1] There is no denying

[1] American revisionists have received encouragement in the present decade from the English historian A. J. P. Taylor, who in his celebrated and controversial book *The Origins of the Second World War* (1961) asserts that Hitler's ambition was confined to Eastern Europe, that he entertained no dreams of spreading Nazi influence across the world. The obvious conclusion to Taylor's logic is that there existed in the late 1930s no evidence that Hitler was a menace to the interests of the United States. One must be cautious, however, in using Taylor to reinforce the revisionist argument, for *The Origins of the Second World War* ends with the eruption

that Hitler wanted to avoid a clash with the United States, that programs such as the destroyer deal and lend-lease were steps toward war, that Roosevelt's assurances to the country were less than honest. This is not to say that the Beard-Tansill school of historians has established the other part of its thesis, that Roosevelt from the outbreak of war in Europe in 1939 tried to maneuver the United States into it. There is scant evidence for this idea, and indeed some against it, such as the President's failure to exploit the *Robin Moor* sinking in spring 1941.

Then there is the view, noted in this chapter, that Roosevelt should have taken the country to war sooner than he did, in spring or summer 1941. Such argument has appeal for the interventionist spirit, but when one recalls the closeness of the vote in the House (212-194) on repeal of the neutrality law's restrictions in November 1941—a vote that came after the affairs of the *Robin Moor, Kearny,* and *Reuben James*—one wonders if Roosevelt's fear of the isolationists was not well taken. The War of 1812 had proved the folly of going to war when a large minority of the population opposed it. Moreover, as events in the Pacific were about to prove, the United States was not ready to fight in 1941, and that being the case it would have been irresponsible as well as foolish to take the country to war.[2]

Which leads to perhaps the most cogent criticism of Roosevelt's leadership in 1939-41. Although the President knew that the

---

of hostilities in September 1939. When the German attack on Poland, contrary to Hitler's hopes, resulted in war with Britain and France, the conflict in Europe doubtless took on a new dimension insofar as the United States was concerned. In a word, if, as Taylor says, Hitler was no threat to American interests before September 1939 it does not necessarily follow that he remained a non-threat after September 1939.

[2] In 1967 there appeared a book by the writer T. R. Fehrenbach, entitled *F. D. R.'s Undeclared War, 1939 to 1941,* which argues, like the revisionists, that Roosevelt indeed was trying to maneuver the United States toward the European war in 1939-41, but unlike the revisionists Fehrenbach contends that such a policy was in the best interest of the United States. In his view Roosevelt did not execute his policy with consummate skill, in part because of excessive concern for his popularity: "A truly great President and American would have no concern for what might happen to him personally once he had committed the nation on an irrevocable course, anymore than a soldier charging up a hill." One may note that initial reviews of Fehrenbach's book were not highly favorable.

war probably would engulf the United States, American mobilization in those years was wheezing along on one cylinder. As late as summer 1941 factories were increasing the output of consumer goods, and the following autumn, as the country edged toward war in the Atlantic, popular magazines carried color advertisements of 1942 automobile models. As mentioned, the string of defeats in the Pacific in the months after Pearl Harbor were saddening testimony to the country's unpreparedness. Defeat in the Pacific was not the only consequence. It took two years to mobilize American war industry after Pearl Harbor, thereby forcing a cautious initial strategy in the war that weakened the Anglo-American position *vis-à-vis* the Soviet Union and opened the way for the eventual communist takeover in Eastern Europe. Indeed it is almost a truism that many of America's frustrations after the Second World War derived from the country's weakness at the time it entered the war.

FIVE

To Pearl Harbor

Of the Japanese attack on Hawaii in December 1941, Robert E. Sherwood *(Roosevelt and Hopkins)* several years later wrote: "Millions of words have been recorded by at least eight official investigating bodies and one may read through all of them without arriving at an adequate explanation of why, with war so obviously ready to break out *somewhere* in the Pacific, our principal Pacific base was in a condition of peacetime Sunday morning somnolence instead of in Condition Red." Many Americans in the 1940s and after shared Sherwood's amazement, and in this atmosphere of historical bafflement perhaps the appearance of a devil theory was inevitable—a theory that Pearl Harbor was a monstrous plot hatched in the dark recesses of Washington.

According to the conspiracy idea, Roosevelt by 1940-41 was

afire with one thought, to take the United States to war with Germany. His purpose? To save Britain and Russia and increase his own prestige and power. The destroyer deal and lend-lease were part of the presidential scheme to provoke Hitler. But the dictator would not accommodate the President by declaring war. Whereupon Roosevelt, ever the Machiavelli of American politics, found the strategy of getting the United States in war against the "real" enemy, Germany, via the "back door." In the words of the revisionist writer Charles C. Tansill *(Back Door to War),* "when the President perceived that Hitler would not furnish the pretext for a war with Germany, he turned to the Far East and increased his pressure upon Japan." War with one Axis power would mean war with the other.

To carry out their design—so revisionists have written—Roosevelt and his fellow-conspirators (Secretaries Hull, Stimson, and Knox, and the army's chief of staff General George C. Marshall) pushed the Japanese to a position where they had to retreat from the Asian mainland to their home islands, or fight. They knew the Japanese would fight. But the master plotters in Washington did not stop there. To unite the country they determined that Japan should strike the first blow, and as a lure for a "sneak" attack—a "stab in the back"—the President exposed the Pacific fleet at Pearl Harbor. The price of presidential treachery? Destruction of two battleships, immobilization of six others, loss of several lesser vessels, elimination of 188 army and navy planes, and the death of 2,403 Americans.

I

The best-known Pearl Harbor revisionists have been Charles A. Beard *(President Roosevelt and the Coming of the War),* Charles C. Tansill *(Back Door to War),* and Harry Elmer Barnes *(Perpetual War for Perpetual Peace).* Others are William Henry Chamberlin *(America's Second Crusade),* George Morgenstern *(Pearl Harbor: The Story of the Secret War,* 1947), Rear Admiral Robert A. Theobald *(The Final Secret of Pearl Harbor,* 1954), and Admiral Husband E. Kimmel *(Admiral Kimmel's Story,* 1955). Like prewar isolationists (which several of them were), revisionists have believed there could be no rational argument against the idea that war in Europe and Asia was not the business of the United States. The President, who was no dupe, understood the isolationist logic, and therefore knew what was best for the country. Still, as Barnes puts it, "to promote Roosevelt's political ambitions and his mendacious foreign policy some three thousand American boys were quite needlessly butchered."

Evidence for the revisionist case is purely circumstantial; no clear-cut documentary proof to support the theory of conspiracy has ever appeared. In the revisionist view the economic boycott of Japan, completed in summer 1941, and Roosevelt's refusal to meet the Japanese prime minister demonstrate that leaders in Washington were seeking war in the Pacific. But the revisionist case centers around Pearl Harbor: the idea that Roosevelt lured the Japanese to Hawaii by exposing the fleet and let the raid come without tipping off army and navy commanders. Revisionists saw that if they could establish this part of their thesis it would be easy enough to accept the argument that Roosevelt was maneuvering the Japanese via diplomacy.

As for Pearl Harbor, revisionists ask questions for which they think there are no satisfactory answers except conspiracy in Washington. Did not intercepted messages (American cryptanalysts had broken Japan's highest diplomatic code, the Purple Cipher) show unmistakable interest in warships at Pearl Harbor, a clear indication of Japanese intentions? What else except conspiracy could explain Secretary Stimson's remark at a White House meeting in November 1941, that the problem of Japanese-American relations was "how we should maneuver them [the Japanese] into the position of firing the first shot"? Why did leaders in Washington fail to provide Hawaii with one of the machines called "Magic" for decoding the Purple Cipher (the Philippines had one), unless they feared that army and navy commanders there would figure out for themselves what was up? And what about the "east-wind rain" code? "Magic" had revealed that the words "east-wind rain" in weather broadcasts would be the Tokyo government's signal to embassies that a break with America was imminent. Revisionists are sure that a monitor picked up the signal but that officials in Washington suppressed the information. Since intercepted messages in the first days of December 1941 indicated that war was about to break out in the Pacific, why did leaders in Washington fail to reiterate the warning to Pacific commanders in the most forceful language—unless Washington wanted surprise? Why did Roosevelt, knowing war to be at hand, fail to send the battleship fleet to sea— unless he wanted it to come under attack? Why were the Pacific fleet's aircraft carriers absent from Pearl Harbor on the fateful Sunday morning? Was it because the President was willing to sacrifice battleships but wanted to save the carriers? And why did General Marshall, on learning from an intercept that a Japanese attack might come at 1:00 P.M. December 7 (Washington time), transmit an alert to Hawaii by commercial telegraph instead of using the "scrambler" telephone on his desk—unless he wanted the message to arrive too late?

In the view of such writers as Herbert Feis (*The Road to Pearl Harbor*), William L. Langer and S. Everett Gleason (*The Undeclared War*), Julius W. Pratt (*Cordell Hull*), Elting E. Morison (*Turmoil and Tradition*), Basil Rauch (*Roosevelt: From Munich to Pearl Harbor*), Walter Millis (*This is Pearl!*), Samuel Eliot Morison (*The Two-Ocean War*, 1963), Forrest C. Pogue (*George C. Marshall, II, Ordeal and Hope*, 1966), Ladislas Farago (*The Broken Seal: "Operation Magic" and the Secret Road to Pearl Harbor*, 1967), and Roberta Wohlstetter (*Pearl Harbor: Warning and Decision*, 1962), the idea of conspiracy has no foundation. Feis, Langer and Gleason, Rauch, and Pratt have shown that each of America's diplomatic moves in the Pacific in 1940-41 was consistent with the Roosevelt administration's estimate of the national interest and requirements of international morality. As for the "back door" thesis, they note that the Axis alliance was defensive, and just as Japan had been under no obligation to declare war when Germany attacked the Soviet Union in June 1941, Germany was under no obligation if Japan should attack the United States. Roosevelt could have had no assurance that a "back door" strategy would take America into the European war. Regarding Pearl Harbor, anti-revisionists (or "court historians," as revisionists contemptuously call them) consider it understandable that the Japanese achieved surprise. Attention in official Washington had been fixed on Southeast Asia and the western Pacific, where Japanese troop concentrations and naval activity indicated a possible attack. In the words of Langer and Gleason, leaders in Washington "had been living from hour to hour with the problem of how to meet the virtual certainty of a Japanese attack in Southeast Asia. . . . Of Hawaii there was apparently no thought. This tragic oversight may be a classic example of human frailty, but it provides no evidence whatsoever to support the thesis that the President or any other responsible American official courted a Japanese attack on the Pearl Harbor base in order to enable them to lead the country into the European War by the Pacific back door."

Regarding revisionist questions about Pearl Harbor, anti-revisionists have nonconspiratorial answers for each. On Japan's interest in ships at Pearl Harbor, intercepts revealed that Japanese agents were collecting information on ships at several points, including the Canal Zone and Singapore; there seemed nothing unusual about interest in those based in Hawaii (although Ladislas Farago, in a chapter entitled "The Missed Clue," thinks a cumulative study by naval intelligence would have revealed a heavier emphasis on ship movements at Pearl Harbor). As for the "east-wind rain" signal, Farago found evidence that Japanese authorities executed it but doubts the testimony of the naval officer (also disputed by other navy men) who said monitors picked it up two days before the raid. On Stimson's "maneuver" statement, Richard N. Current in "How Stimson Meant to 'Maneuver' the Japanese" (*Mississippi Valley Historical Review,* XL, June 1953) contended that Stimson's remark did not prove conspiracy. Anticipating a Japanese strike somewhere in Southeast Asia, the secretary was seeking an announcement, perhaps a presidential declaration, that such a blow would constitute a threat to American interests. If it fell the President could claim that Japan had fired the first shot and ask Congress for war. On failing to provide Hawaii with a "Magic" decoding device: such machines were difficult to assemble, and of course the more machines about, the greater the chance the Japanese would realize that the United States had broken the Purple Cipher.[1] As for giving war alerts, the Washington government had issued commanders a "war warning" on November 27, and as Stimson

[1] One may note that the Philippines had a "Magic" machine, but commanders there did not conclude from intercepts that Pearl Harbor was about to come under attack.

later said *(On Active Service)*, "we assumed that . . . it would not be necessary to repeat that warning over and over again during the ensuing days." As for the President's failure to send the battleships to sea, his naval advisers, thinking nobody could launch aerial torpedoes in a channel as shallow as that at Pearl, believed Hawaii the safest place in the Pacific for the fleet. On absence of the carriers: those "flat-tops" available for duty were off delivering planes for defense of Wake and Midway, under the circumstances a legitimate enterprise. On Marshall's failure to use the scrambler telephone, the general's biographer Forrest C. Pogue says that nobody suggested using the phone: "If anyone had, Marshall would not have risked revealing that the United States had broken the Japanese diplomatic code by relying on the dubious security of the scrambler then in use."

Perhaps Roberta Wohlstetter has given the best explanation, apart from the fixation on Southeast Asia, for failure of leaders in Washington and commanders in Hawaii to read "signals" pointing to an attack at Pearl Harbor: "It is much easier *after* the event to sort the relevant from the irrelevant signals. After the event, of course, a signal is always crystal clear; we can now see what disaster it was signaling, since the disaster has occurred. But before the event it is obscure and pregnant with conflicting meanings. . . . In short, we failed to anticipate Pearl Harbor not for want of the relevant materials, but because of a plethora of irrelevant ones."

To this one might add the view of Ladislas Farago that ability to decode the Purple Cipher filled American leaders in autumn 1941 with a smug feeling of security: "Mr. Roosevelt and his associates . . . assumed that thanks to the 'Magics,' they could learn well in advance everything the Japanese were planning, enabling them to apply whatever preventive or counter measures they deemed advisable and necessary." Thus "Magic" was "partly responsible for the complacency with which the American authorities approached the final crisis in November and December 1941."

Though most historians reject the idea of conspiracy, the question remains of the wisdom of America's Far Eastern policy during the year or so before Pearl Harbor. Using general studies as a measure, the prevailing view parallels that set forth in the writings of Feis, Langer and Gleason, and Rauch, *i.e.,* most historians think the Roosevelt administration made the proper responses to Japanese moves in East Asia in 1940-41. As explained by Feis ("War Came at Pearl Harbor: Suspicions Considered," *The Yale Review,* XLV, Spring 1956): "Our Government did obstruct Japanese efforts, believing them to be unjust, cruel, and a threat to our national security, especially after Japan became a partner with Hitler's Germany and Mussolini's Italy and bent its efforts toward bringing the world under their combined control." As for the revisionist idea that Roosevelt forced Japan into war by unreasonable demands, Feis *(The Road to Pearl Harbor)* retorts that it is absurd to claim that compliance with American demands would have meant extinction of Japanese nationality. The United States insisted that Japan give up no territories or resources except those held by force. The Japanese government would have remained independent and there would have been no limits on Japanese military power. In Feis's words, "extinction threatened the plan for expansion in Asia, but not Japan or the Japanese."

Not everyone agrees. While rejecting the conspiracy theory, a few writers have considered America's policy in the Far East in 1941 poorly conceived, claiming that it brought a war in the Pacific which the United States with honor and profit might have avoided. The first clear expression of this view appeared in 1952 in the memoirs of Joseph C. Grew *(Turbulent Era),* America's ambassador to Japan in 1932-41. Books by the British scholar Francis C. Jones *(Japan's New Order in East Asia,* 1954) and Paul W. Schroeder *(The Axis Alliance and Japanese-American Relations,* 1958) have offered support. According to these men, the United States and Japan in 1941 might have struck a truce: Japan breaking away from the Axis alliance and pledging no new aggression in East Asia, the United States lifting restrictions on trade with Japan. As for other issues, including Japan's presence in China, they could await outcome of the war in Europe. Instead, the United States insisted on total surrender—withdrawal from the East Asian mainland to the home islands. Japan of course had invested too much blood and treasure in the China adventure to make such a retreat.

The Grew-Jones-Schroeder thesis is a heady wine and a large draught can send the imagination soaring. If the government in Washington could have postponed a showdown in the Far East the

United States could have put all its strength in the balance against Hitler. Not only would the European war have ended sooner; the Anglo-American armies could have gone ashore in France a year or so before they did, swept eastward, and saved much of Eastern Europe from the Red Army and communism. After defeating Hitler the triumphant Allies could have wheeled around to the Pacific and compelled the Japanese, perhaps without a fight, to disgorge their empire. The deadly campaigns on Guadalcanal and Iwo Jima would never have taken place, the United States would not have gained the dubious distinction of dropping the first atomic bomb, and spared from continuous fighting Chiang Kai-shek's government in China might have brought the regeneration of Chinese life that would have kept the world's most populous country out of the communist orbit. And Japan? Though wounded in pride, it would have remained a force in the Far East, a bastion against the Soviet Union and the ideas of communism. A heady wine indeed!

II

After the *Panay* affair of December 1937 the Japanese, according to Herbert Feis *(The Road to Pearl Harbor),* "went deeper into the stubble," extending control in North China and winning the principal Chinese coastal areas. Step by step the imperial armies were fulfilling the vision of a "new order" in East Asia resting on Japanese hegemony in China.

In the United States a public clamor arose in early 1939 for the government to do something (nonviolent, of course) about China, whereupon the President in July performed a maneuver to satisfy the popular urge for action and give pause to the Japanese: he ended the Treaty of Commerce and Navigation (1911). In six months—January 1940—the United States would be free to limit or terminate exports to Japan—free to impose sanctions if Japan joined the Axis and continued aggression in East Asia. Or, as the revisionist Charles C. Tansill *(Back Door to War)* later saw it, "the way was thus prepared for an all-out economic offensive against Japan." Knowing that Japanese imperialism relied on American oil and scrap metal, Roosevelt hoped the Tokyo government might relax pressure in China rather than risk an economic boycott. If events in Europe in August-September 1939 left no time for self-congratulation, the President had cause for satisfaction over his move in the Far East. Termination of the trade treaty brought applause all across the American nation and in Tokyo the leaders of Japan betrayed alarm lest the United States discard verbal protest in favor of sanctions.

Still, there was no weakening of Japan's determination to put together a Greater East Asia Co-Prosperity Sphere. Japanese armies continued to advance in China, air squadrons droned on, and European and American business came under new attack. The Tokyo government also planned a puppet regime for China, to be located in Chiang Kai-shek's former capital of Nanking, and increased the pressure of a diplomatic drive begun earlier in the year to persuade the British and French to get out of China. The Japanese, however, were anxious to smooth over any difficulties with the United States, and repeatedly assured American diplomats that once they resolved the "China incident" the trade door would swing open and everybody, including the Chinese, would enjoy the rewards of Japan's imperialism.

Soothing words from the Foreign Office in Tokyo (Tansill referred to them as "gestures of conciliation") drew little response in Washington. The United States was under no illusions about Japan's "new order." The Greater East Asia Co-Prosperity Sphere would be a closed system, geared to function to Japan's advantage. And China? It would become a giant vassalage. In the view of some Americans the best step would be a boycott of Japan, a move that would end America's shameful suckling of Japanese armies and bring national policy in line with moral principle. To that end several bills came before Congress in January 1940, but President Roosevelt decided against sanctions. Senator Tom Connally of Texas, anxious to punish Japan, complained that "we fired a few blank cartridges and then fell back."

The President had reason for caution. Sanctions might provoke the Japanese, and the United States was not ready for a fight. Even if the threat of war passed there was nothing to suggest that Japanese armies would stop dead in their tracks for want of American supplies. More likely leaders in Tokyo would turn to Southeast Asia. There was, moreover, the war in Europe. Action that raised the temperature of affairs in the Pacific would be inimical to any

American plans for helping fight Hitler. Roosevelt concluded that the best policy was to leave the lines of trade undisturbed while searching for new ways to bolster China. On the latter point the problems were acute, for China's finances were near collapse and Japanese control of Chinese ports required that most supplies find their way to Chiang Kai-shek via the tortuous Burma Road.

The Japanese meanwhile had run into difficulty. War maps in Tokyo did not project China's vastness; the countryside seemed to swallow imperial armies. Nor was success crowning their attempt to persuade Chiang Kai-shek that Japan's imperialism would benefit China; the Chinese leader continued to refuse the hand of Japanese friendship. In their frustration leaders in Tokyo decided to go through with establishing the puppet regime at Nanking. Perhaps Chiang in time would come to his senses. There was some concern lest the United States respond with a boycott, but establishment of the Nanking government in March 1940 brought nothing more from Washington than a denunciation.

Then Hitler, in spring 1940, ended the "phony war" in Europe. One of his first victims was the Netherlands, and the Foreign Office in Tokyo buzzed with the question of what would happen to the Dutch East Indies, one of the world's richest sources of oil, rubber, tin, bauxite, nickel, and manganese. Would the Germans claim them? Or would the British attempt a "preventive" occupation?

Secretary of State Cordell Hull also wondered about the Dutch colony, but his main concern there was a Japanese takeover. He surmised, accurately, that Japan's plan for a "new order" in East Asia included the Netherlands Indies, and to dissuade them from moving to the area he reminded the Japanese that in 1922 they had agreed "to respect the rights of the Netherlands in relation to their insular possessions in the region of the Pacific Ocean." He warned that a disturbance in the East Indies would endanger peace in the entire Pacific, and to reinforce the secretary's words President Roosevelt ordered the Pacific fleet from San Diego to Pearl Harbor. It developed that the Japanese were in no hurry. Assured that neither the Germans nor the British would occupy the islands, they were content with a Dutch pledge (June 1940) of no interference with the trade line that fed East Indian supplies to Japan.

Meanwhile, Hitler's strike westward in Europe had commanded the energies of France and Britain, leaving their Asian colonies almost defenseless. Would the poverty-ridden Japanese, seeing the world of the Occidentals turning upside down, satisfy their national urge for treasure and grandeur by carrying the Rising Sun to Indochina, Malaya, and Burma? The answer seemed affirmative, for even before Germany had swept over France the Tokyo government began to yank the cords of diplomacy, warning the British that they could avoid trouble in the Far East only by closing the Burma Road and sealing the border between Hong Kong and the Chinese mainland. At the same time they demanded that the French close the Indochina frontier and grant Japan the right to keep a control commission in the French colony. To show that they meant business the Japanese sent warships to thrash about in the Gulf of Tonkin, and made military demonstrations along the Indochina border.

Some Japanese believed these policies too meek. In their view the opportunity to cash in on Hitler's victories in Europe was too dazzling to let pass, especially when one measured a strike southward against the only alternative: carrying on the dreary, endless war in China. In the words of one prominent Japanese: "We should not miss the present opportunity or we shall be blamed by posterity." Charging that the present government had moved too slowly down the road destiny had marked out for the Japanese nation, militants demanded a bolder policy, declaring that the Western democracies had no choice but to yield to Japanese ambition. Japan should cast away its fear of America, join the Axis alliance, and stake out a claim to Southeast Asia by helping Hitler achieve his great purpose of overpowering Britain.

Amid these stentorian calls to national greatness Tokyo early in July 1940 began to reverberate with rumors of the imminent downfall of the cabinet. The threat of assassination hung over the capital and there were whispers that militant conspirators would not spare Emperor Hirohito if he opposed a cabinet change. A fortnight later the army crudely handed the government an eviction notice. The prime minister of the new government was Prince Fumimaro Konoye, a former prime minister, who had family connections in the palace and a wide popular following. A genial man, Konoye had a fondness for America but was on good terms with the army and not apt to oppose its will. In charge of the Foreign Office was a conceited and impulsive demagogue, Yosuke Matsuoka, the man who at the League of Nations in 1933 had defended Japan's occupation of Manchuria. Another key official was the war minister, General Hideki Tojo, known as "Razor Brain" because of his quick intelligence. In a matter of days the new government set out its policy: an end to the war in China, a firm policy toward the United States, alliance with the Axis, better relations with the Soviet Union, and more vigorous diplomacy in Southeast Asia.

Warning lights by now were flashing in Washington, not because of the cabinet change in Tokyo so much as the sudden increase in Japanese purchase of aviation gasoline and lubricants. Did the build-up signal a military expedition to Southeast Asia? Or were the Japanese storing oil for war against the United States? Whatever the reason, American leaders decided the time had come for a stronger stand, and the President, claiming that America's national defense required new efforts to stockpile strategic materials, imposed an embargo on the sale of aviation gasoline and top-grade scrap iron to Japan. Although the embargo affected only a fraction of the traffic in scrap metal and oil between North American ports and the other side of the Pacific, it served notice to the Japanese that there were limits to the patience of the United States.

Unimpressed by America's show of firmness, the Konoye government began to prod the Dutch. The main object was an increase in the flow of oil and other materials from the Netherlands Indies to Japan, and to that end leaders in Tokyo demanded the right to send a special mission to the colony to discuss economic matters. Other plans were less obvious. The Japanese had decided to try to cut the ties of the Indies to the Netherlands. Achieving that, they would coerce authorities in the Indies to recognize Japanese supremacy in the islands. The Dutch saw through Japanese intentions and managed to keep concessions to a minimum.

The Japanese also turned up the pressure on Indochina, and in August 1940 demanded the right to send troops across Tonkin province and build airfields in the northern reaches of that colony. Though they insisted that their only purpose was to engineer defeat of Chiang Kai-shek and prevent elements hostile to Japan from taking over the country, the Japanese foxes in truth were seeking entrance to the Indochinese chicken coop. The French looked to the United States for help, but leaders in Washington declined to make any promises pending a trend in the air battle going on over Britain. The French government at Vichy then toyed with the idea of resisting the Japanese. Perhaps in the steaming jungles of Southeast Asia the arms of France could recover some of the luster lost in the recent humiliation by the Germans. Such thoughts were mere flights from reality, and after securing a pledge that Japan would respect French sovereignty the doors of Indochina opened and late in September 1940 several thousand imperial soldiers took up station in the colony.

Japan meanwhile edged toward alliance with the Axis. As was perfectly apparent, the object of a Rome-Berlin-Tokyo pact would be the United States. Rather than risk a two-theater war, so Hitler and Mussolini hoped, the United States might stand apart from the conflict in Europe and permit Britain to go down to defeat. For the same reason some Japanese militants thought the Americans would submit to Japanese supremacy in East Asia.

Not all Japanese leaders were convinced, however, and an air of misgiving settled over the Japanese capital as negotiations went forward. The emperor took a gloomy view of Hitler, and the navy, fearful of war with America, saw the alliance as provocative. Undeterred, the army and other militants pressed on. They held the levers of power, it turned out, and their will prevailed. Negotiations ended in late September 1940, when representatives of Germany, Italy, and Japan gathered in Berlin and signed the Tripartite Pact amid ceremonies climaxed by what Hans L. Trefousse (*Germany and American Neutrality*) describes as "the godlike entry of the Führer." The signatories recognized Japanese supremacy in East Asia, German-Italian supremacy in Europe, and all of them pledged to support any of the others that came under attack.

Alarmed by events in the Far East, the United States in September 1940 decided on an embargo of all scrap metal to Japan, not just the "top-grade" material. The embargo—announced the day before Japan joined the Axis—came as a blow to Tokyo's imperialists. Loss of American scrap meant that the Japanese would have to redouble their own efforts to build steel-producing facilities. They would also have to find new sources of iron ore and coking coal (three tons of ore and coking coal were required to turn out the equivalent of one ton of scrap metal). The resulting strain on the country's manpower, machinery, and shipping would be serious.

Would Japan retaliate against the embargo, denounced by the government in Tokyo as an "unfriendly act"? After holding their breath for several days leaders in Washington began to debate new measures to contain Japanese imperialism. Some of the President's advisers counseled a "hard line"; others opposed intimidation, warning that the navy was not prepared to fight Japan. After weighing all arguments, Roosevelt decided on a "middle way." He would keep up pressure on the Japanese but try not to excite them to new violence. To that end he set about co-ordinating Far Eastern policy with the British, and gave increased attention to Chiang Kai-shek, in late 1940 apparently near the end of his resistance. Roosevelt arranged a new loan to China, promised Chiang fifty modern fighter planes, and took steps to provide passports to American nationals who wanted to fly in Chiang's air force. Meanwhile he ordered a handful of planes, ships, and submarines sent to the Philippines, then extended the ban on exports to Japan (in Tansill's view, an enlargment of Roosevelt's "economic offensive"), ending traffic in iron ore, pig iron, steel, and many types of tools.

III

The advent of the year 1941 promised no moratorium on America's difficulties in the Far East. In the first month of the new year the Japanese set out to tighten their grip on Indochina and renewed efforts to get a foothold in the Netherlands Indies. They also were at work on other fronts, pushing their influence in Siam, a strategic center in Southeast Asia, by sponsoring Siamese claims to territory in Indochina, and sounding out the Soviets on the possibility of an accord that would assure the northern frontier of the Japanese empire.

At this point, in January 1941, Roosevelt received Bishop James E. Walsh and Father James M. Drought of the Maryknoll mission society, just back from Tokyo, and for two hours listened to a "peace proposal" that Foreign Minister Matsuoka had outlined to them the previous month. As they understood it, the proposal had originated with Prime Minister Konoye. It seemed to suggest an agreement whereby Japan would support the United States in event of a German attack; Japanese troops would leave China after termination of the "China incident" on "the basis of the secret truce terms offered last October by Chiang Kai-shek," the Open Door would reappear in China, and the United States would provide economic assistance to both Japan and China.

In the words of Julius Pratt (*Cordell Hull*), "the offer, had it been official and in good faith, would have gone far to satisfy American aims in the Far East and to detach Japan from her Axis partners." That was the trouble. An expression of the views of Japanese moderates, it was not official (according to Hull's memoirs, it was not even new) and the State Department doubted that any government in Tokyo could implement such a proposal. It did not, moreover, contain any pledge of restraint in Southeast Asia, leading Roosevelt and Hull to the conclusion that, in the unlikely event the Japanese did agree to leave China, they would merely increase the pressure in Indochina, Siam, and the Netherlands Indies.

Whatever the government's reasons for not giving credence to the "proposal," revisionists have seen the episode as another justification for their theory that Roosevelt was seeking war with Japan. In the words of Tansill (Harry Elmer Barnes, ed., *Perpetual War for Perpetual Peace*), "thus ended an anxious effort on the part of the Japanese government to find a path to peace." Then with shocking crudeness Tansill concludes: "It seems quite possible that the Far Eastern Military [War Crimes] Tribunal brought to trial the wrong persons. It might have been better if the tribunal had held its sessions in Washington."

His attention still centered on Europe, Roosevelt decided to continue the policy of firmness tinctured with caution in the Far East. He urged the Dutch to maintain their stand against the Japanese, then as a warning to the Tokyo government sent squadrons of warships on cruises to the western Pacific, where they called at the Philippines, Australia, and New Zealand. He bolstered American defenses in Guam and extended the embargo list, adding such items as copper, brass, bronze, zinc, nickel, potash, phosphate, and uranium.

At this point the Japanese sent a new ambassador to the

United States, Admiral Kichisaburo Nomura, who took up residence in Washington in February 1941. In Tansill's view this was "another friendly gesture" by Japan, for Nomura, an intense man of modest intellect, thought well of Americans, having been assigned to Washington during the First World War. There was hope in Tokyo that Nomura would head off trouble between the United States and Japan and at the same time persuade American leaders to examine Japanese avenues of thought about East Asia. Unfortunately Nomura was not free to follow his own instincts, and before many weeks it was clear that he was a puppet manipulated by the Foreign Office in Tokyo. Still, in the absence of anything more constructive it seemed like a good idea to talk with Nomura, and beginning in March 1941 the new ambassador and Secretary Hull had regular conversations, usually in the quiet atmosphere of Hull's apartment at the Carlton Hotel.[2]

The pattern of the Hull-Nomura talks became fixed at the first meeting, and over the next nine months the ambassador and secretary had little that was new to say to one another. Or as Hull later put it in his memoirs, talks with Nomura always seemed "to come to a certain point and then start going around and around in the same circle." Over and over Nomura repeated the tired argument that Americans did not understand Japanese intentions; that by nature the Japanese were not warlike; and only in face of harassment and injustice by such "satisfied" powers as Britain and the United States had Japan decided that imperialism was the road to national salvation. As for an understanding, that was possible if the United States would restore trade with Japan, help the Japanese obtain materials (oil, bauxite, tin, etc.) in Southeast Asia, press Chiang Kai-shek to accept Japanese terms for peace, stop supporting Chiang if he rejected such pressure, and assist Japan in diplomatic maneuvers against the British in Southeast Asia. For their part the Japanese would limit themselves to peaceful persuasion in Southeast Asia and keep to the letter of the Tripartite Pact, supporting Hitler only if Germany came under attack.

---

[2] One may note that Germany strongly opposed the Hull-Nomura conversations. According to Hans L. Trefousse (*Germany and American Neutrality*), "were these to succeed, Japan's value [to the Germans] as a diverting influence on Washington would sink to nil."

Japanese proposals amounted to exchanging pawns for rooks and knights on the chessboard of East Asia, and American leaders never for a moment considered accepting them. Still, Hull avoided an unqualified rejection, keeping up the pretense that the United States might make concessions. His aim was to avert a showdown in the Pacific while storm clouds were swelling over the north Atlantic, the focal point of American interests in spring-summer 1941. Otherwise he made clear his belief that over the previous decade Japan had been guilty of aggression, treaty-breaking, and violation of the principle of self-determination. He advised that the only sure way to effect peace and stability in East Asia was for the Japanese to withdraw from the mainland to their home islands.

While gazing eastward across the Pacific for some clue that the Americans might change their stand against a "new order" in East Asia, Japanese diplomats also looked westward, to Moscow. Unaware that their Nazi partners had decided to consign the Russo-German nonaggression pact of 1939 to oblivion, leaders in Tokyo were still seeking some kind of neutrality agreement with the Soviets. Their idea was to strengthen Japan in China and Southeast Asia by eliminating the danger of a Russian blow at the Japanese flank. To strike an agreement with the Soviets, Foreign Minister Matsuoka left Tokyo at the end of February 1941, boarded a train at Vladivostok, and set out across the plains of Siberia on the long journey to Moscow.

After a cordial hearing in the Soviet capital Matsuoka went off to Berlin to inform his Axis allies as to his aims. Hoping that Japan would join the war against the Soviet Union, only three months in the future, the Germans disliked Matsuoka's design for a Russo-Japanese neutrality pact, but decided against telling the talkative foreign minister what they had in mind for the Russians. The Soviets meanwhile, having caught a scent of German intentions, decided that they too had a flank to secure, the eastern one opposite the Japanese empire. When Matsuoka returned to Moscow in April 1941 they agreed to the Russo-Japanese neutrality pact, pledging peaceful relations and respect for each other's territory.

Not many weeks afterward, on June 22, 1941, German armies invaded the Soviet Union. The Germans expected the Japanese to join the fight against the Russians and Matsuoka was anxious to oblige. Other Japanese leaders were opposed. Since the Tripartite Pact was only a defensive arrangement, the Japanese were under no commitment to support Hitler's attack; Japan's obligation was to respect the Russo-Japanese neutrality agreement. Matsuoka's opponents also noted that a campaign against the Soviets would divert men and weapons from the Chinese front, postponing a conclusion of the "China incident." And what rewards awaited Japan in the eastern reaches of the Soviet Union? Siberia was a wasteland; Japan should keep its attention on the treasurehouse of Southeast Asia. In any event the Germans probably would defeat the Russians without Japanese help in a few months, and after Russia's collapse the British would have to make peace with Hitler. With Britain out of the war the Americans would have to come to terms with the Axis, and in the grand division of spoils Japan would become master of East Asia.

In the first days of July 1941 the Japanese charted their policy. They would not join Hitler's war against the Soviets unless unfolding events held out promise of new advantage. They would continue to concentrate on Southeast Asia, and in a few weeks imperial troops would complete the takeover of Indochina. The emperor's agents meanwhile would step up the campaign to make Siam a puppet state, and from the Indochina-Siam base the Japanese would put fresh pressure on Malaya and the Netherlands Indies. Such a policy, of course, was a repudiation of Matsuoka, and a cabinet shuffle later in the month brought a new foreign minister, Admiral Teijiro Toyada, a more pliant man and one who supposedly stood high with the Americans.

Thanks to "Magic" ("Magic's" finest hour, according to Ladislas Farago in *The Broken Seal*), leaders in Washington knew of Japanese plans, but knowledge did little to relieve the agony of deciding what America's response should be. Clearly the United States could ill afford merely to look on while Japan took Indochina and Siam, and just as clearly the country's first concern was the war in Europe. Unfortunately the United States did not have the means to stand up against the Nazis in the north Atlantic and fight the Japanese in the western Pacific. The problem facing American leaders, then, was how to resist Japanese aggression without provoking active hostilities.

After extensive consultation President Roosevelt decided to "freeze" Japanese funds already in the United States. A freezing order would place Japanese-American trade under presidential control, for only a license issued from Washington could release "frozen"' Japanese dollars to pay for transactions in the United States. Should the Japanese refuse to back off from Indochina, the President could retaliate by refusing licenses. If he chose he could terminate all commerce between the United States and Japan, a punishment the Japanese could ill afford. Despite restrictions of the previous year, trade with America remained essential to Japan's prosperity. And, as everybody knew, American oil was the life-blood of the Japanese military mechanism.

But what if the Japanese refused to give way before America's economic pressure? What if a boycott provoked them to attack Malaya and the Netherlands Indies? Or even the United States? Roosevelt saw that a freezing order would be risky, that it might provoke a war in the Pacific that he hoped to avert or at least delay. But he believed Japan's lunge in southern Indochina would so threaten American interests that a strong response was mandatory.

When news reached Washington on July 24, 1941 that troop transports flying the Rising Sun were steaming toward Saigon in the southern part of Indochina, the President drafted an order freezing Japanese assets. But before executing it he decided to give diplomacy one more chance by hearing out Ambassador Nomura. Roosevelt rejected Nomura's argument that the move southward in Indochina intended to prevent "encirclement" of the Japanese empire by an Anglo-American-Dutch combine; but he promised that if Japan jettisoned the present maneuver he would do everything possible to achieve neutralization of Indochina. On the evening of July 25, when it became apparent that the diplomatic exchange had accomplished nothing, the President's office announced the freezing order. The next day the governments of Britain and the British Dominions also imposed financial controls on commerce with Japan and two days later the Dutch government-in-exile in London followed.

No historian has minimized the importance of the freezing order. William L. Langer and S. Everett Gleason (*The Undeclared War*) have written that it was "probably the crucial step in the entire course of Japanese-American relations before Pearl Harbor." The order, which over the next few weeks became the instrument for ending virtually all trade between America and Japan, was an open challenge to Japanese imperialism. In the words of Herbert Feis (*The Road to Pearl Harbor*), it compelled Japan "to choose between making terms with us or making war against us." T. R. Fehrenbach (*F.D.R.'s Undeclared War, 1939 to 1941,* 1967) describes the freezing order as "the most severe form of economic warfare." Although most historians refrain from criticizing the order, apparently seeing it as a proper if dangerous response to Japan's move in southern Indochina, David J. Lu in *From the Marco Polo Bridge to Pearl Harbor: Japan's Entry into World War II* (1961) thinks the freezing order was a mistake. Arguing that "in applying economic sanctions, the timing is important," he concludes that "to have been effective, the embargoes should have been imposed immediately after the outbreak of hostilities in China [*i.e.* in 1937]. Otherwise they should have been delayed indefinitely." To revisionists, of course, the freezing order was another move in fulfillment of Roosevelt's design for war, Charles C. Tansill (*Back Door to War*) noting that on the day before he announced the order the President rejected another "gesture of good will" by the Japanese. The "gesture" was not a suggestion that Japan might scrap plans for grabbing Indochina, but a communication by a Japanese emissary that there was a chance of amicable settlement if the United States refrained from freezing Japanese funds.

A fortnight later President Roosevelt and Britain's prime minister Winston Churchill had their "Atlantic Conference" off the coast of Newfoundland. In their discussions they ranged over the problem of Japanese expansion, and revisionists—particularly Charles A. Beard (*President Roosevelt and the Coming of the War*) and George Morgenstern (*Pearl Harbor: The Story of the Secret War*)—have insisted that Roosevelt committed himself to an ultimatum that the United States would resist "any further encroachment" by Japan in the southwestern Pacific, even at risk of war. Beard considered this one of the "actualities of the Atlantic Conference," obscured by Roosevelt's public pronouncement that he had made no pledges to Churchill, *i.e.* by the "appearances" of the conference. Basil Rauch (*Roosevelt: From Munich to Pearl Har-*

bor) has gone to some length to refute the revisionist contention, arguing that Roosevelt and Churchill never considered an ultimatum to Japan (only a warning) and made no commitments (merely "exchanged information of their intention to issue warnings to Japan"). Whatever one thinks of Rauch's debate with the revisionists over semantics, it is hard to quarrel with his conclusion that Roosevelt watered down America's statement "until in its final form it was a rather mild warning that if Japan failed to accept an unconditional American offer to renew conversations, and committed new aggressions, the United States would take steps to protect its interests and security."

In Japan meanwhile there was confusion and dismay. The Japanese had expected some response to the move to southern Indochina but the freezing order was more than they had bargained for. What should they do? Retreat before Anglo-Dutch-American pressure was unthinkable. That left one alternative: to avoid economic strangulation Japan must bring the wealth of Malaya and the Netherlands Indies into the Japanese empire. Such a move, however, would very possibly mean war with the United States, and only a few hotheads in the army felt enthusiasm for a clash with that power.

In their frustration Japan's leaders turned to diplomacy, but offered little more than a promise to send no more troops to Indochina and to withdraw from the French colony when the "China incident" ended. In return they wanted the United States to restore normal trade with Japan, help bring Chiang Kai-shek to terms, and recognize Japan's special position in Indochina. Referring to this period of Japanese-American relations, the revisionist Harry Elmer Barnes (*Perpetual War for Perpetual Peace*) wrote that "Japan veritably crawled on its diplomatic belly . . . to reach some workable understanding with the United States." If Japanese proposals represented important concessions, then American diplomatists were dolts who missed the point.

The Japanese next proposed a meeting between Prince Konoye and President Roosevelt. The President at first expressed interest, but Secretary Hull persuaded him that such a meeting offered no advantage. Hull was certain that the Japanese prime minister could make no concessions. Indeed, by raising false hopes in the United

States that a settlement with Japan might be imminent, a meeting might be worse than useless. Still, Roosevelt thought it a good idea to string the Japanese along, and through September 1941 kept alive Konoye's hopes. Konoye meanwhile had a specially outfitted steamer, *Nitta Maru,* standing by at Yokohama, ready at a moment's notice to sail to a rendezvous with the American President.

The proposal for a Konoye-Roosevelt meeting has become a popular topic of historical discussion. The revisionist George Morgenstern (*Pearl Harbor: The Story of the Secret War*) has written that "Roosevelt was being offered the chance that might have avoided war. He chose to refuse it." Charles C. Tansill (*Back Door to War*) takes a stronger view. He thinks the United States should have conceded Japan's dominance in East Asia in autumn 1941; that it should have seen that "in the Far East the future belonged either to Japan or Russia, not to a China that had been exhausted by an endless cycle of war, revolution, and war." A realistic appraisal, Tansill contends, would have produced a decision to accept Japan as a barrier to the Soviets and their communist ideas. Instead the United States elected to support China, and "the later collapse of the American position in China stems straight back to the decisions taken in September and October 1941." As for a Konoye-Roosevelt meeting, Tansill writes that when the President turned it down "he had cleared the decks of the American ship of state for war at any time."

No revisionists, Francis C. Jones (*Japan's New Order in East Asia*) and Paul W. Schroeder (*The Axis Alliance and Japanese-American Relations*) also think Roosevelt ought to have met Konoye. They accept the view of Ambassador Grew, expressed in impassioned notes to the State Department from August-September 1941, that a meeting of the two leaders might have produced a temporary settlement—perhaps a lifting of trade restrictions in return for Japan's pledge to make no new moves southward. A final settlement of Far Eastern issues, including the question of Japan's presence in China, could have awaited the result of the war going on in Europe. A similar view comes from David J. Lu (*From the Marco Polo Bridge to Pearl Harbor*). Agreeing with Jones and Schroeder that an agreement between the United States and Japan was possible, Lu thinks that a Roosevelt-Konoye meeting, if accomplishing little else, would have set back the timetable of the Pearl Harbor raid. The inference is that given more time the two powers might have worked out their differences.

The Jones-Schroeder argument has found little response among other non-revisionist historians. Herbert Feis (*The Road to Pearl Harbor*) thinks Konoye had nothing to offer the President, hence a meeting would have achieved nothing. Langer and Gleason (*The Undeclared War*) agree: "The Japanese might be divided on the question of what direction and method to choose for expansion and conquest, but there is no evidence that any important figure, civilian or military, was prepared to abandon aspirations which were truly national." Noting that Konoye, to secure their consent for a meeting, had promised military leaders that he would insist on "the firm establishment of the Greater East Asia Co-Prosperity Sphere," Julius W. Pratt (*Cordell Hull*) writes: "It seems reasonable to suppose, therefore, that Hull was correct in assuming that only through a surrender by the United States could a Roosevelt-Konoye meeting result in an agreement." Waldo H. Heinrichs (*American Ambassador*) writes that Ambassador Grew "tended to a more hopeful view of things than circumstances warranted," and like the foregoing writers doubts that Konoye had any latitude for concessions. Also believing that Grew was bemused by Konoye's talk of moderation, Heinrichs agrees with Langer and Gleason that "the moderates of August and September 1941, no less than the Army and Navy, desired economic invulnerability and East Asian leadership for Japan. However, they were more subtle, flexible, patient, and wary."

IV

By late August 1941 the nerves of the Japanese nation were becoming increasingly taut. One reason was oil. The Americans and the Dutch, first on one pretext and then another, had turned off the flow of petroleum products to Japan, compelling the Japanese to dip into precious reserves. At the same time the great British base at Singapore was receiving reinforcements, and to the east the Americans had improved fortifications at Guam and brought to the Philippines a squadron of B-17 bombers, the far-ranging "flying fortresses" which recently had proved themselves in the European war. As Japanese militants sized up the situation, Konoye's time for achieving victory in East Asia by diplomacy was running out.

September replaced August and militants determined to set plans for war with America in motion. When they took their thoughts to the emperor, he recalled that the army in 1937 had promised a quick victory over China; but he gave in when the navy chief compared Japan with a patient suffering a critical illness: drastic surgery might produce death, but offered the only chance of saving the patient's life. In deference to the emperor's hope that diplomacy might yet achieve a peaceful solution, the militants agreed to give Konoye a few more weeks. If in that time his bloodless methods failed they would make ready to release Japan's power in November or December, the last period for many months when weather would favor the kind of operations they had in mind.

The key areas in the militants' design were Java, Sumatra, Borneo, and Malaya, a vast territory rich in oil, rubber, tin, rice, bauxite, iron ore, and manganese. To bring them under control the Japanese had to overcome two obstacles, the American B-17 bombers in the Philippines and British ships and planes at Singapore. By cunning they believed they could knock over both obstacles. Regarding Singapore, its big guns pointed out to sea, the British never having considered anything but a frontal attack. The Japanese planned to land troops far up the Malay peninsula and send them southward through the jungle, striking Singapore from the rear. In the Philippines, if there were no Japanese aircraft carriers in the South China Sea the Americans would consider their bombers safe, for according to American calculations the Philippines were beyond range of bombing planes at Japan's nearest base, Formosa. To destroy the B-17's the Japanese would devise means of bringing the Philippines within range of Formosa, launch a surprise attack, and catch the "flying fortresses" on the ground.

How would Japan protect its enlarged empire? The Japanese were counting on their Axis allies to support the drive to Malaya and the Netherlands Indies by declaring war on the United States. But they knew that in the end protection would be up to them. A first step in defense of the empire, they decided, would be destruction of the American Pacific fleet, based at Pearl Harbor in Hawaii. The fleet ought to be an easy target for a surprise attack from the air. America's attention would be riveted on Japanese moves seven thousand miles west of Hawaii, in Southeast Asia; the Americans did not have the aircraft necessary to effectively patrol Hawaiian waters, and American naval people thought the shallow channel at Pearl Harbor protected their ships from aerial torpedoes. Thus the Japanese had to keep the Americans focused on Southeast Asia, take care not to "telegraph" the strike at Hawaii, and put into operation new techniques for launching aerial torpedoes in shallow water. While the American fleet was immobilized Japanese soldiers would take over and occupy the Marianas, Carolines, Gilberts, Marshalls, Bismarcks, Solomons, and Philippines (or such of those islands as they did not already occupy), as well as the Netherlands Indies, Malaya, Siam, and Burma, establishing a defensive perimeter stretching southward from the Kuriles through the central Pacific and westward across Southeast Asia to the gates of India. From their maze of island bases the Japanese could then annihilate any task force that tried to get through. After several years of watching their sailors and airmen perish in futile attempts to breach Japan's defenses the Americans, also struggling against Hitler, would grow weary of the fight and accept a settlement recognizing Japanese supremacy in East Asia.

Konoye meanwhile continued his diplomatic efforts, but the piles of dispatches, memoranda, and statements yielded no hope that the United States and Japan might resolve their differences. The Japanese would consider nothing beyond murky promises of a strict interpretation of the Tripartite Pact, *i.e.* they promised not to join their European partners in war against the United States except in event of American aggression. The United States wanted pledges of an early Japanese withdrawal from Southeast Asia and China. Japan would consider such a withdrawal only after "satisfactory" conclusion of the "China incident."

If Japanese moves in Southeast Asia had touched off the crisis in Japanese-American relations in 1941, it was clear by autumn 1941 that China was a main obstacle to settlement in the Far East. Paul W. Schroeder (*The Axis Alliance and Japanese-American Relations*) believes this was unfortunate and unnecessary. He writes that down to July 1941 the United States had "sought to attain two limited objectives in the Far East, those of splitting the

Axis and of stopping Japan's advance southward." Both objectives, Schroeder thinks, were within reach. Then, "on the verge of a major diplomatic victory, the United States abandoned her original goals and concentrated on a third, the liberation of China." According to Schroeder, "this last aim was not in accord with American strategic interests" and "was completely incapable of being achieved by peaceful means."

One may make several observations about Schroeder's argument. First, Japanese leaders never intimated that they might consider a settlement without reference to China. Proposals emanating from the Foreign Office consistently listed resolution of the "China incident" as a condition of any agreement with the United States, and when the special envoy to Washington, Saburo Kurusu, proposed a truce in November 1941 that would have left the China question in abeyance he received a sharp rebuke from Tokyo. Also, American leaders were less committed to the idea of liberating China than Schroeder suggests. Kurusu's overtures sparked interest in Washington and late in November 1941 Secretary Hull drafted a proposal for a *modus vivendi* similar to that outlined by the Japanese envoy. "Magic" having reported the Tokyo's government's rebuke to Kurusu, Hull concluded that such a proposal had no chance, and in face of rumors that he and Roosevelt were considering a "sellout" of China dropped the idea.

When Konoye in mid-October 1941 reached the end of his tether—when it became clear that he would achieve no diplomatic agreement with the United States—he and his cabinet resigned. The new prime minister was General Tojo, the small soldier who had helped guide the adventure in China. In asking Tojo to form a government the emperor explained that it was the imperial will that the new cabinet continue the search for peace, and Tojo's biographer Robert J. C. Butow (*Tojo and the Coming of the War*) has written that war was not the purpose of the new first minister: "He became premier in order to break the deadlock of indecision which had threatened to prevail indefinitely under Konoe [sic]."

When the passing days gave no promise of a peaceful solution, Tojo and his militant associates determined to act. The result was a five-hour meeting on November 5, 1941 in which civil and military leaders, in the imperial presence, set out Japan's course.

To appease the emperor Japan would play the diplomatic game a few weeks longer, but if new overtures to the United States yielded no accord by November 25, the government would ask the emperor's sanction for an attack. The Tokyo government meanwhile would seek promises from Germany and Italy that they would follow Japan to war against the United States, although everybody agreed that Japan should not purchase help by proclaiming hostilities on the Soviet Union. Later that same day Japanese army and navy commanders learned that "war with Netherlands, America, England inevitable; general operational preparations to be completed by early December." Two days later Japanese leaders fixed the date for attack at December 8, 1941, Tokyo time.

While American leaders listened in via "Magic," the Tokyo government warned Ambassador Nomura of the November 25 deadline for an accord with the United States. There was no mistaking the inference that after that date the Japanese would strike. The government also advised that in response to Nomura's appeal, made the previous August, an experienced diplomat in a few days would fly to Washington to help with negotiations. The new man was Saburo Kurusu, a friend of Nomura and a former ambassador to Germany. As for instructions on how to continue the diplomatic effort, leaders in Tokyo directed Nomura first to submit so-called Plan A and if, as expected, it met rejection he was to present Plan B.

Nomura handed "Plan A" to Hull on November 10. Like the replay of a worn recording, the latest Japanese missive called for the United States to restore normal trade with Japan and try to persuade Chiang Kai-shek to meet Japan's terms for peace. If Chiang refused the United States was to stop all aid to China. For their part the Japanese would guarantee an "open door" to trade in their empire—when all other parts of the world accepted that principle. They would evacuate troops from China—after establishment of peace and "the lapse of a suitable interval." They would evacuate Indochina—after conclusion of the "China incident." They would observe the letter of the Tripartite Pact—would attack the United States only if the United States attacked the European Axis. Without ceremony the American government rejected "Plan A."

Knowing that his mission was "window dressing," Kurusu arrived in Washington a few days after the demise of "Plan A." He carried no new instructions and was aware that his government was about to pull the switch that would signal war. Still, he determined, in his words, to try to score a "touchdown" for peace. After huddling with Nomura he concluded that the best prospect was a truce that would give the governments in Washington and Tokyo time to cool off. His idea was to return to the *status quo ante* July 1941— Japan would get out of southern Indochina and the United States and its allies would lift trade restrictions. Such ideas aroused guarded interest among the Americans. The reaction in Tokyo, as mentioned, was different. A few days later "Magic" revealed that leaders of Japan had rejected Kurusu's plan and rebuked the new envoy for exceeding instructions.

Nomura on November 20 placed "Plan B" before Hull. If the language was cloudy, the meaning was clear. Japan would pledge no new moves in Southeast Asia and the western Pacific and would withdraw from Indochina after a general settlement. The United States would unfreeze Japanese assets, supply Japan with "a required quantity of oil," press the Dutch to reopen the East Indies to trade with Japan, and discontinue support of Chiang Kai-shek. It was the final paragraph that assured rejection of "Plan B," for under no circumstances was the United States prepared to terminate aid to China. According to Feis, "whoever insisted on the last paragraph—Tojo and the Army certainly did—insisted on war." Samuel Eliot Morison ("Did Roosevelt Start the War? History Through a Beard," *Atlantic Monthly*, 182, August 1948) has written that the concessions demanded in "Plan B" were "appropriate for a nation defeated in war."

Refusing to let peace die because they had grown weary of the search for terms, Hull and his staff at the State Department worked long hours in the days before the deadline of November 25 to work out a truce, a *modus vivendi* that would allow the United States and Japan more time. Knowing there could be no compromise on the China problem, the State Department decided, *a la* Kurusu, to propose a return to the situation as it had been before July 1941. Japan would withdraw from southern Indochina and the United States would rescind the order freezing Japanese funds.

The United States would put no pressure on Chiang Kai-shek but would not look with disfavor on Sino-Japanese negotiations.

As Hull and his staff labored on, they learned from "Magic" that after November 29 "things are automatically going to happen." Since that date was only a few days away, it was clear there was not enough time to work out a truce. Still, there seemed some advantage in going through the motions of proposing a last-minute armistice; posterity would see that America had sought peace to the very end. That idea died when the Chinese, catching the rumor of a "deal," calculating that any agreement would be at their expense, submitted urgent appeals that the United States accept no terms that might compromise China's interests. American newspapers friendly to Chiang Kai-shek took up the cry, and corridors and cloakrooms of Congress buzzed with talk that the State Department was drafting a sellout of China. Lest it receive interpretation as such a sellout, Hull persuaded Roosevelt to drop the *modus vivendi* proposal. Looking back on these events a decade later, Langer and Gleason (*The Undeclared War*) conceded that there was virtually no chance of saving the peace in late November 1941. They thought nonetheless that Roosevelt and Hull should not have abandoned the *modus vivendi* "when there was still a glimmer of hope that Tokyo might accept it."

Apparently for the sake of the historical record, Hull on November 26 secured the President's approval for a "ten-point" proposal, which he submitted to the Japanese envoys later in the day. A reiteration of principles that Japan had refused many times, the proposal was sure to elicit a rejection. According to the revisionist Charles A. Beard (*President Roosevelt and the Coming of the War*) this was an ultimatum, although in diplomatic parlance an ultimatum carries the threat of action in event of refusal. The ten-point proposal threatened nothing.

Serene in the belief that he had done everything possible, Hull wrote Stimson on November 27: "I have washed my hands of it, and it [the situation] is now in the hands of you and Knox, the Army and Navy." That same day a "final alert" went out to commanders in the Pacific, the message to Admiral Husband E. Kimmel at Pearl Harbor reading: "This dispatch is to be considered a war warning. Negotiations with Japan looking toward stabilization of conditions in the Pacific have ceased and an aggressive move by Japan is expected within the next few days." Revisionists, including Beard, Kimmel (*Admiral Kimmel's Story*), and Robert A. Theobald (*The Final Secret of Pearl Harbor*), have referred to this communication as a "so-called war warning."

In Tokyo preparations were underway to play out the final ritual. The government learned late in November that the European Axis would declare war if new Japanese maneuvers brought a clash with the United States.[3] Relieved that Japan would not have to fight

[3] Hans L. Trefousse (*Germany and American Neutrality*) explains that Hitler's policy throughout 1941 was to avoid war with the United States while Japan diverted American attention to the Pacific. The Germans were uneasy about any "departure from the Nazi practice of taking on one enemy at a time," but were powerless to prevent the Japanese from attacking the United States. And if Hitler "wanted to keep the Island Empire as an ally, he had to agree to war with America." James V. Compton, *The Swastika and the Eagle: Hitler, the United States, and the Origins of World War II* (1967) agrees that Hitler wished to keep the United States occupied in the Pacific, but does not see the Germans as hoping for restraint by the Japanese: "In the face of abundant evidence that a Japanese expansion to the south would, in all likelihood, provoke an American military reaction, the Germans pressed their allies toward aggression." Saul Friedländer in *Prelude to Downfall: Hitler and the United States, 1939-1941* (1967) takes a similar view, citing German Foreign Minister Joachim von Ribbentrop's enthusiastic assertion on December 9, 1941 that Japan's attack on the United States was "the most important event since the beginning of the war."
But would it not have been possible for the Germans, while encouraging the Japanese in their quarrel with the United States, to have stopped short of a pledge to follow their Axis partner to war against the North American power? Conceivably Hitler could have left the Japanese to fight the Americans by themselves—just as the Japanese had left the Germans to fight the Soviets. To these points one can cite the view of Compton and Friedländer that Hitler believed a declaration of war on the United States at this time was a formality, that American policy in the Atlantic already had created a state of war. Then one might add that the accounts by Trefousse, Compton, and Friedländer seem to suggest another motive for German promises to follow Japan to war with the United States: failure to give such assurances might have persuaded the Japanese to call off the attack, open new discussions with the Americans, and reach a settlement that would enable the United States to turn away from the Pacific and concentrate exclusively on Europe.
Still, from the vantage of German interests did the need of maintaining the Axis alliance and preventing a Japanese-American détente balance the risks inherent in war with the United States? Was Hitler not reducing his chances of final victory by taking on another enemy at this time? To these questions one can respond with Friedländer's view that Hitler thought war between Germany and the United States was imminent, irrespective of

alone, the national leaders on December 1 met in the imperial presence to submit the decision for war. Tojo presided. The emperor uttered not a word, his face expressionless. Silence in such affairs amounted to assent. The remaining question was whether Japan should strike before breaking off diplomatic negotiations. To preserve the chance of surprise the generals and admirals wanted to continue the diplomatic charade to the last moment. Civil members of the government believed that Japanese honor would suffer irreparable harm if the attack came without warning. As a compromise military and civil leaders agreed that Nomura and Kurusu should cut the cords of diplomacy twenty minutes before Japanese planes roared down on American targets—a warning, but too late to alert defenders.[4]

V

In Washington, as late autumn breezes swirled leaves across the White House lawn, American leaders glumly awaited the Japanese blow. They knew from "Magic" that the Foreign Office in Tokyo had directed its embassies to burn diplomatic codes, a sure sign of war. Another intercept reported the Foreign Office's instructions to the Japanese ambassador in Berlin. He was to advise the Germans "that there is an extreme danger that war may suddenly break out between the Anglo-Saxon nations and Japan through some clash of arms and that the time of the start of this war may be quicker

---

what the Japanese might do. Hence the questions in truth were academic. Moreover, according to Friedländer, Hitler in late 1941 believed the entire war would turn on the outcome of the fighting in the Soviet Union. It would be many months, perhaps a year or more, before the United States could bring much power to bear against its European enemies. Thus if the Germans could quickly smash the Red Army and then turn the full might of the *Wehrmacht* to the West, at the same time organizing the vast territory from the Urals to the Atlantic, they likely would be able to hold off the Anglo-Americans and force a negotiated settlement that would leave Hitler as master of Europe. Friedländer thinks the dictator's calculus was correct, that a German victory in Russia probably would have secured Hitler dominance on the Continent—unless the war had dragged on and America's atomic bomb, finally perfected in 1945, had tipped the scales against him.

[4] As it turned out, Nomura and Kurusu, because of confusion at the embassy in Washington, did not deliver the message ending negotiations until more than an hour after the first bombs had fallen on Hawaii.

than anyone dreams." The Americans also knew that two large fleets of Japanese cruisers, destroyers, and transports were rounding the southern tip of Indochina, their destination apparently Malaya or Siam.

The historian Raymond A. Esthus ("President Roosevelt's Commitment to Britain to Intervene in the Pacific War," *Mississippi Valley Historical Review*, L, June 1963) thinks evidence from British and Commonwealth sources proves that Roosevelt had given "Britain a commitment of armed support in the case of a Japanese attack on British or Dutch territory or on Thailand." And the record, as put together from American sources, is clear that Roosevelt in early December 1941 had determined to ask Congress for war if the Japanese attacked Malaya or the Netherlands Indies. But if the Japanese moved to Siam or made a new attack on China (there was talk that Japan might try to close the Burma Road by striking from Indochina into Yunnan province) he was less confident that he could rally the country for war. Whatever the problems, he began to draft a message to Congress outlining American interest in Southeast Asia, which was a device for warning the Japanese that new aggression on their part might bring a clash with America, and also for conditioning the United States to the prospect of hostilities. He planned to deliver the message on December 8.

While the President worked on his message and a last-minute appeal to the Japanese emperor urging peace, "Magic" on December 6 began to decode a long communication to Nomura and Kurusu; it was the Tokyo government's reply to the ten-point proposal of November 26. Thirteen parts of the fourteen-part message went to the White House that evening. Reading the intercept, the President said, without emotion: "This means war." After breakfast the next morning—Sunday, December 7—Roosevelt received the fourteenth part. It announced that because of "the attitudes of the American government" there was no chance of agreement through negotiation.

Later that morning "Magic" decoded another intercept, this one marked "Urgent—Very Important." It directed Nomura to submit Japan's reply to the ten-point proposal promptly at one o'clock that afternoon. This last piece of intelligence indicated that something might break in the Pacific at that hour. Advised by his office that important information had come in, General Marshall, after his usual Sunday morning horseback ride, hurried to the War Department building. After consulting Admiral Harold R. Stark by phone he decided to send a new alert to San Francisco, the Canal Zone, Hawaii, and the Philippines. He dispatched the message via the army's message center, the channel least likely to tip off the Japanese that the United States had broken the Purple Cipher. Encoded, the message went out by radio within thirty minutes. Operators quickly got through to San Francisco, the Canal Zone, and the Philippines, but because of atmospheric interference could get no response from Hawaii. Unaware of the urgency of Marshall's communication, the signal officer in charge of the message center now sent the warning to Hawaii by Western Union. Some two hours later in Oahu a messenger, a Japanese-American youth wearing a green shirt and khaki pants, picked up a batch of cables. One was addressed to "Commanding General," Fort Shafter. As the young man steered his motorcycle toward the army base his eye caught sight of anti-aircraft bursts over Pearl Harbor.

Toward the end of October 1941 a large part of the imperial Japanese fleet returned to the home islands.[5] While stevedores loaded most ships with equipment for operations in a tropical climate, *i.e.,* Southeast Asia, thirty-three of the vessels—carriers, battleships, cruisers, destroyers, and tankers—took on winter gear. To one of the ships, the giant carrier *Akagi,* workmen delivered a large crate. Inside was a mock-up of the American naval base at Pearl Harbor. Also receiving attention were twenty-seven of Japan's *I*-class submarines. More than three hundred feet long, these were the finest submarines in the world. Five of the big underwater boats were specially rigged to carry two-man "midget" submarines.

Aboard the *Akagi* a handful of top officers pulled apart the

[5] The following account rests on Walter Lord, *Day of Infamy* (1957); John Deane Potter, *Yamamoto: The Man Who Menaced America* (1965); Andrieu D'Albas, *Death of a Navy: Japanese Naval Action in World War II* (1957); Masanori Ito, *The End of the Imperial Japanese Navy* (1962); Kazuo Sakamaki, *I Attacked Pearl Harbor* (1949); Masatake Okumiya and Jiro Horikoshi, *Zero!* (1956); Walter Millis, *This is Pearl!* (1947); and U. S. Congress, Joint Committee on the Investigation of the Pearl Harbor Attack, 79th Cong., 1st Sess., Part 13.

crate containing the mock-up of Pearl Harbor. Studying the model with particular intensity were Commander Minoru Genda, a young and talented staff officer who was in charge of the projected air strike against the American base, and Lieutenant Commander Mitsuo Fuchida, the veteran flier who would lead the Pearl Harbor Attack Air Groups. At scattered locations through Japan, meanwhile, air crews—the cream of the Japanese naval air arm—completed a long period of simulated attacks on stationary targets, then, summoned by Genda, made their way to the *Akagi*. When they assembled Genda rolled out maps of the island of Oahu in the Hawaiian chain, showed them the mock-up of Pearl Harbor, and explained that they would attack American vessels resting at their moorings (hence the practice in hitting non-moving targets).

On November 10 those *I*-class boats not carrying midget submarines began, in groups of three, to leave their berths at Kure and Yokosuka. Eight days later those with midgets slipped into the Pacific, destination Hawaii. That same day, November 18, the thirty-three surface vessels, one by one, weighed anchor, steamed far out to sea, then swung northward toward Tankan Bay in the Kurile Islands. En route to their rendezvous the ships kept radio silence. To deceive American monitors radio operators still in port tapped out a stream of fake messages which gave the appearance that no task force had departed. Adding to the deception, large parties of sailors from Yokosuka Naval Barracks went to Tokyo on sightseeing tours. Naval leaders hoped that foreign observers in the capital would take note.

Tankan Bay, in Etorofu, largest of the Kuriles, was a gloomy, forsaken place in November 1941. Snow capped the peaks that surrounded the harbor, walrus and seals sprawled lazily on the beaches. On a small concrete pier were thousands of drums of oil, and sailors shivered as they loaded these on ships and lashed them to decks. Meanwhile in briefing rooms of the *Akagi,* flagship of the fleet, the task force's commander, Vice Admiral Chuichi Nagumo, fifty-seven years old, a veteran of many years in the imperial navy, went over plans with subordinate commanders and airplane crews. The aviators were enthusiastic, commanders subdued. The latter knew that if the mission were to succeed the task force would have to plow across 3,000 miles of open sea without being detected.

Complicating the operation would be the problem—about every three days—of maneuvering tankers alongside warships for refueling, a hazardous business in the cold, choppy waters of the north Pacific.

At length everything was set and on November 25 Admiral Isoruku Yamamoto, the renowned leader who the previous January had begun to plan the Pearl Harbor strike, back at imperial naval headquarters, personally radioed the order to proceed. That night three submarines which would range 200 miles ahead of the task force, watching for merchantmen that might tip off the Americans, moved out. At dawn the following morning Admiral Nagumo from the bridge of the *Akagi* gave the sign, signal lights blinked, and through a dense fog the task force slipped out of the harbor into the icy waters of the north Pacific. The course was almost due east—outside the lanes normally used by commercial vessels. To avoid detection the flotilla maintained radio silence. Rigid orders forbade the dumping overboard of garbage and other waste. When emptied, oil drums went into storage. Firing the ships' boilers was the best quality fuel oil—to keep down smoke. At night the fleet observed a total blackout. What were these elaborate precautions all about? Why were they cruising in this northern latitude? Ordinary seamen wondered. They reckoned that they must be on some sort of special maneuver.

While pilots memorized every terrain feature of the island of Oahu, studied silhouettes of American ships, went through calisthenics, Admiral Nagumo, a grim, thick-set man, paced the bridge of the *Akagi,* worried lest he receive orders to turn back. Anxiety ended on the night of December 2 when an officer knocked at the admiral's door and handed him a message from imperial headquarters: "Climb Mount Niitaka." A mountain in Formosa, Mount Niitaka was the highest peak in the Japanese empire and the message was the signal to go ahead with the attack. Next day, as the task force steamed 900 miles north of Midway, ship captains summoned men to top decks and over loudspeakers announced that the fleet's objective was Pearl Harbor. Cries of "Banzai!" pierced the Pacific air. Seamen wept. Many wrote letters home, one man scribbling: "An air attack on Hawaii! A dream come true!" Another composed a poem.

After holding the same easterly course a few hours longer Nagumo's ships veered to the southeast. At this point the sea became heavy, gale-force winds lashed the task force, huge waves swept several men overboard. The ships did not pause. When fog settled over the flotilla, raising the danger of collision, there was no order to reduce speed. On the morning of December 6, as the sea continued to churn, the tankers refueled the warships for the last time, then, amid sentimental farewells, fell away from the striking force.

As it pressed down on the island of Oahu the fleet received a radio message from Yamamoto: "The moment has arrived. The rise or fall of our empire is at stake." Ships captains again ordered men to top decks. Their voices blaring excitedly over loudspeakers, the captains read Yamamoto's communication, then issued their own patriotic calls to greatness. Seamen cheered. Up the mast of the *Akagi* went the same flag that had flown over Admiral Heihachiro Togo's flagship *Mikasa* during annihilation of the Russian fleet in the Tsushima Straits in 1905. As the flag whipped in the wind the men of the great carrier spontaneously broke forth with the Japanese national anthem. From the bridge of the *Akagi,* Nagumo now ordered full speed ahead: twenty-four knots. Radio operators monitored broadcasts from stations KGU and KGMB in Honolulu for any hint that the Americans had detected the task force. All they heard were the melodies of Hawaiian ballads and routine programs. The only distressing note came from Tokyo, a coded message that the aircraft carriers of the American Pacific fleet presently were absent from Pearl Harbor.

Several hundred miles to the south the submarine fleet already had taken position around Oahu. In addition to launching the midget submarines for an underwater sortie inside Pearl Harbor, the *I*-class boats were to sink any American ships that tried to escape after the assault from the air. When darkness settled over the Pacific the submarines rose to the surface. Seamen could see neon lights flashing in Honolulu, some could hear the strains of music drifting out from Waikiki Beach. In five of the vessels there was grumbling. Crews of the midget submarines resented the order restraining their attack until the airplanes had made the first run at the American fleet.

Meanwhile, through the night of December 6-7 (Honolulu time) Nagumo's task force plowed through the swelling sea. Few men slept. Then at 5:00 A.M., Sunday, December 7 crews began final preparations. Darkness still enveloped the fleet. At 5:30 two seaplanes catapulted to the air to make a final reconnaissance of Pearl Harbor and soon the six "flat-tops" were alive with the roar of engines as mechanics made last-minute adjustments. On lower decks airmen nervously slipped into clean uniforms, checked goggles, helmets, and other personal gear. Some carefully wrapped about themselves *hashimaki* headbands, traditional symbols that the wearers must be prepared to die. Others knelt before little Shinto shrines, sipped ceremonial draughts of *sake,* prayed that heaven would bless their mission. Next a quick breakfast, then a final briefing.

A few minutes before six o'clock the airmen moved up to flight decks. Air crews on the *Akagi* lined up facing the ship's bridge and on receiving the formal command to carry out orders dashed to their planes. The carriers now were swinging in a giant arc, turning their noses into the north wind. As Commander Fuchida in the lead aircraft, a high-level bomber, was pulling on his helmet a mechanic leaped to the wing, handed him a red and gold turban made of silk, and asked: "Sir, may I offer you this with respect, from the mechanics?" Fuchida accepted the gift, wrapped it around his head, then started his engine. Like a string of firecrackers other motors coughed to life and within seconds the planes that were to go as the first wave were poised, engines screaming, blue flame spitting from cowlings. His turban flapping in the wind made by his propeller, Fuchida peered down the flight deck. The sky was black, pale blue lights marked out the runway. The commander now closed the canopy of his aircraft. At the end of the deck the control officer, holding a green lamp, moved his arm in a circle. As the carrier rocked and pitched, Fuchida's plane lurched forward, roared down the flight deck, and took to the air. One by one, from all six carriers, the fighter planes (the famous *Zeroes*), dive bombers, torpedo planes, and high-level bombers repeated the maneuver, 183 aircraft in all. Sailors cheered them on their way with cries of "Banzai!" At 10,000 feet the planes assembled for the attack. Pearl Harbor lay 230 miles to the south and slightly west.

As the air squadron droned toward Pearl Harbor at 146 miles per hour, Fuchida in the lead plane noted heavy cloud formations. He feared he might find the target blanketed. Then, about seven o'clock, the clouds parted and out of the eastern sky a shimmering morning sun beamed across the Japanese planes. Visibility would be perfect. Forty minutes later the commander, peering into the distance, could see the surf breaking against a shoreline, Kahuku Point, Oahu. On reaching the point the attacking force divided, one group peeling off for an attack on the American army's air base, Wheeler Field, near the center of the island, the other, under Fuchida, proceeding toward Pearl Harbor, on the south coast of Oahu. As the lush Hawaiian countryside passed beneath his wings, Fuchida pondered another question: which group of attackers should he send first against the American ships, torpedo planes or dive bombers? It would be better to lead with the torpedo planes, letting them launch their missiles before dive bombers spoiled targets. But the torpedo planes were slow and would make easy targets if the Americans had learned of the attack. In the event his squadron had lost the element of surprise, therefore, he would dispatch the dive bombers first and hope that the confusion created by their assault would afford some protection for the torpedo planes.

Minutes later Fuchida and his airmen could see Pearl Harbor. They expected anti-aircraft fire. There was none. No American interceptor planes rose to meet them. And spread out below in neat alignment were main elements of the American Pacific Fleet, including eight battleships. Amazed, Fuchida wondered if the Americans ever had heard of Japan's surprise attack on the Russian naval base at Port Arthur in 1904, the first action of the Russo-Japanese War.

Fuchida then pulled back the canopy of his plane and fired a single "black dragon" signal flare to indicate that the attack was a surprise. The honor of striking the first blow at the American fleet had fallen to the lumbering torpedo planes. Taking aim on "battleship row," the planes swooped to sea level, headed straight for the giant dreadnoughts, released their torpedoes, and banked sharply away. But thinking some pilots had missed his signal, Fuchida had fired a second "black dragon." Two flares were the signal for "surprise lost." Seeing the second flare, dive bomber pilots thought the commander wanted them to go in first and they screamed to the attack. Thus, as Walter Lord writes, "in a welter of confusion, the High Command's plan for carefully integrated phases vanished."

Whatever the confusion in the sky over Pearl Harbor, America's isolation now belonged to history.

A Note on Historiography

There are several books that describe most of the events covered in this volume. The best is Selig Adler, *The Uncertain Giant: American Foreign Policy Between the Wars* (New York, 1965), a thoughtful analysis resting on a massive study of primary and secondary works. Robert A. Divine, *The Reluctant Belligerent: American Entry into World War II* (New York, 1965) is a survey of American policy from 1933 to Pearl Harbor that is particularly good for the period 1939-41. Allan Nevins, *The New Deal and World Affairs, 1933-1945* (New Haven, 1950) traces American foreign relations from Franklin D. Roosevelt's inauguration to the end of the Second World War. A volume in the *Chronicles of America,* it is exceptionally readable. Another useful survey is Jean-Baptiste Duroselle, *From Wilson to Roosevelt: Foreign Policy of the United States, 1913-1945* (Cambridge, Mass., 1963). For the influence of economics on American policy in the 1930s there is Lloyd C. Gardner, *Economic Aspects of New Deal Diplomacy* (Madison, Wis., 1964), a book that assumes the reader is grounded in principles of economics. Two critical surveys of American diplomacy in the 1930s are Charles A. Beard, *American Foreign Policy in the Making, 1932-1940* (New Haven, 1946) and Charles C. Tansill, *Back Door to War: Roosevelt Foreign Policy, 1933-1941* (Chicago, 1952). Although Beard and Tansill were competent scholars, few historians take seriously their work on diplomacy in the Roosevelt years. So intense was their dislike for the President that they seemed unable to view events of the period with any detachment. The student of American diplomacy must not overlook George F. Kennan, *American Diplomacy, 1900-1950* (Chicago, 1951). A historian as well as a diplomat, Kennan has set down in this volume his reflections on American diplomacy in the first half of the present century. The book is a small masterpiece. William E. Leuchtenburg, *Franklin D. Roosevelt and the New Deal, 1932-1940* (Chicago, 1963) is another reference for this period.

Several memoirs, diaries, and biographies touch the subject of the present book at a number of points. Among the memoirs the most useful is the two-volume *Memoirs of Cordell Hull* (New York, 1948). Sometimes Hull's memory was faulty—a weakness of most memoirs—and sometimes he exaggerated his own influence. Still, the Hull volumes offer many insights to the problems and rationale of American policy in the years before Pearl Harbor. After Hull's the most important memoir is Henry L. Stimson and McGeorge Bundy, *On Active Service in Peace and War* (New York, 1947). The Stimson memoir is particularly valuable for the periods 1931-33 and 1940-41. Other helpful memoirs are Sumner Welles, *The Time for Decision* (New York, 1944), William Phillips, *Ventures in Diplomacy* (Boston, 1952), and Hugh R. Wilson, *Diplomat Between Wars* (New York, 1941). See also Harry S. Truman, *Memoirs by Harry S. Truman, I, Year of Decisions* (Garden City, 1955). The reader who can manage the Japanese language might consult the memoirs of Prince Fumimaro Konoye (or Konoe). Of published papers, the most useful for this study is Walter Johnson (ed.), *Turbulent Era: A Diplomatic Record of Forty Years, 1904-1945,* 2 vols. (Boston, 1952), the papers of Joseph C. Grew. Less satisfactory is Joseph C. Grew, *Ten Years in Japan* (New York, 1944). An important diary is John M. Blum (ed.), *From the Morgenthau Diaries,* 2 vols., *Years of Crisis, 1928-1938* (Boston, 1959) and *Years of Urgency, 1938-1941* (Boston, 1965). Then there is Nancy Harvison Hooker (ed.), *The Moffat Papers: Selections from the Diplomatic Journals of Jay Pierrepont Moffat* (Cambridge, Mass., 1956). The most important biography concerning American diplomacy in the decade before Pearl Harbor is Julius W. Pratt's two-volume *Cordell Hull* (*The American Secretaries of State and Their Diplomacy,* XII, XIII, New York, 1964). Resting in part on Hull's private papers, the Pratt volumes present a readable account of the Tennessean's diplomacy. Another valuable biography is Elting E. Morison, *Turmoil and Tradition: A Study of the Life and Times of Henry L. Stimson* (Boston, 1960), the only full-scale biography of Stimson. See also the essays on Hull and Stimson in Norman A. Graebner (ed.), *An Uncertain Tradition: American Secretaries of State in the Twentieth Century* (New York, 1961). For American relations with Japan one should consult the splendid biography by Waldo H. Heinrichs, *American Ambassador: Joseph C. Grew and the Development of the United States Diplomatic Tradition* (Boston, 1966).

There is no monographic treatment of America's desire for peace in the years between the wars. For insight into some of the favorite proposals of the peace movement—such as disarmament—consult Dexter Perkins, *America's Quest for Peace* (Bloomington, Ind., 1962), a collection of essays by one of the country's outstanding scholars of diplomacy. The analysis of the peace movement and its origins appears in the chapters by Alexander DeConde and Robert H. Ferrell in DeConde (ed.), *Isolation and Security: Ideas and Interests in Twentieth Century American Foreign Policy* (Durham, N.C., 1957). Selig Adler's *Isolationist Impulse: Its Twentieth Century Reaction* (New York, 1957) offers additional information on views and activities of American pacifists. See also *The Man in the Street: The Impact of American Public Opinion on Foreign Policy* (New York, 1948). For the idea that the United States was not an isolationist country in the 1920s see William Appleman Williams, "The Legend of Isolationism in the 1920's," *Science and Society* (Winter 1954). The definitive account of the movement to outlaw war is Robert H. Ferrell, *Peace in Their Time: The Origins of the Kellogg-Briand Pact* (New Haven, 1952). For study of the Nye Committee investigation there is John E. Wiltz, *In Search of*

Peace: The Senate Munitions Inquiry, 1934-36 (Baton Rouge, 1963). One might get a feeling for the pacifist mood in the 1930s by looking at some contemporary books: Helmuth C. Engelbrecht and Frank C. Hanighen, *Merchants of Death: A Study of the International Armament Industry* (New York, 1934); George Seldes, *Iron, Blood and Profits: An Exposure of the World-Wide Munitions Racket* (New York and London, 1934); and Charles A. Beard, *The Devil Theory of War; An Inquiry into the Nature of History and the Possibility of Keeping Out of War* (New York, 1936). An excellent study of the writers who in the 1920s and 1930s criticized American entry in the World War is Warren I. Cohen, *The American Revisionists: The Lessons of Intervention in World War I* (Chicago, 1967). Samuel Lubell, *The Future of American Politics* (New York, 1952) explains American isolationism in the interwar years in ethnic terms, a view challenged by Manfred Jonas in *Isolationism in America, 1935-1941* (Ithaca, N. Y., 1966). The best account of the anti-war movement in the last years before Pearl Harbor is Wayne S. Cole, *America First: The Battle Against Intervention, 1940-1941* (Madison, Wis., 1953). For a partisan account of the activities of American interventionists in 1939-41 see Walter Johnson, *The Battle Against Isolation* (Chicago, 1944).

The Manchurian affair of 1931-33 has been the object of considerable study. Of the book-length accounts two deserve mention. The first to appear was Henry L. Stimson, *The Far Eastern Crisis: Recollections and Observations* (New York, 1936). Secretary of state during the crisis, Stimson defended his policy in his book. Armin Rappaport, *Henry L. Stimson and Japan, 1931-1933* (Chicago, 1963), has sought to balance sympathy for Stimson's purpose with criticism of the consequences of his policy. Generally unsatisfactory is Sara R. Smith, *The Manchurian Crisis, 1931-1932* (New York, 1948). The most lucid analysis of American policy in Manchuria appears in Robert H. Ferrell, *American Diplomacy in the Great Depression: Hoover-Stimson Foreign Policy, 1929-1933* (New Haven, 1957). Unlike many other students, Ferrell takes a generous view of Stimson's efforts in Manchuria. See also Ferrell, *Kellogg; Stimson (The American Secretaries of State and Their Diplomacy,* XI, New York, 1963). For another friendly appraisal there is Elting E. Morison, *Turmoil and Tradition,* already mentioned. For a critical analysis consult Richard N. Current, *Secretary Stimson: A Study in Statecraft* (New Brunswick, N.J., 1954). See also A. Whitney Griswold, *The Far Eastern Policy of the United States* (New York, 1938); Herbert Hoover, *The Memoirs of Herbert Hoover*, I, *The Cabinet and the Presidency* (New York, 1951); and Richard N. Current, "The Stimson Doctrine and the Hoover Doctrine," *American Historical Review*, LIX, 1953-54. To understand United States policy toward Japan in the years 1931-41, the student might examine one of the surveys of American dealings with Japan: William L. Neumann, *America Encounters Japan: From Perry to MacArthur* (Baltimore, 1963) and Edwin O. Reischauer, *The United States and Japan* (Cambridge, Mass., 1957). Two excellent books discuss the effect of the Manchurian affair on politics in Japan: Takehiko Yoshihashi, *Conspiracy at Mukden: The Rise of the Japanese Military* (New Haven, 1963) and Sadako N. Ogata, *Defiance in Manchuria: The Making of Japanese Foreign Policy, 1931-1932* (Berkeley, 1964). See also Yale Candee Maxon, *Control of Japanese Foreign Policy: A Study of Civil-Military Rivalry, 1930-1945* (Berkeley, 1957). All of the last three books rest on extensive research among Japanese sources. For contemporary accounts see Owen Lattimore, *Manchuria: Cradle of Conflict* (New York, 1932) and Kiyoshi K. Kawakami, *Manchukuo: Child of Conflict* (New York, 1933).

Franklin D. Roosevelt entered the White House in March 1933 and his first important act in foreign affairs came during the London Economic Conference. The best account of the conference appears in Herbert Feis, *1933: Characters in Crisis* (Boston, 1966). Consult also Arthur M. Schlesinger, Jr., *The Age of Roosevelt*, II, *The Coming of the New Deal* (Boston, 1966), and Broadus Mitchell, *Depression Decade: From New Era Through New Deal, 1929-1941* (New York, 1947). Much attention in the years 1933-37 centered on the neutrality debate. The best account is Robert A. Divine, *The Illusion of Neutrality* (Chicago, 1962). The neutrality legislation of 1935 and 1936 also receive treatment in John E. Wiltz, *In Search of Peace*, mentioned above. Several senators played large parts in the neutrality discussion, and three are subjects of biographies: Wayne S. Cole, *Senator Gerald P. Nye and American Foreign Relations* (Minneapolis, 1962), Marian C.

McKenna, *Borah* (Ann Arbor, 1961), and Fred L. Israel, *Nevada's Key Pittman* (Lincoln, Neb., 1963). Interesting but, because of many errors, of limited value are the memoirs by Burton K. Wheeler, *Yankee from the West* (Garden City, 1962) and Tom Connally, *My Name is Tom Connally* (New York, 1954). Observations on American relations with Nazi Germany appear in William E. Dodd, *Ambassador Dodd's Diary, 1933-1938* (New York, 1941). A focal point in foreign affairs in the mid-1930s was the war between Italy and Ethiopia. For American policy toward the conflict in East Africa see Brice Harris, Jr., *The United States and the Italo-Ethiopian Crisis* (Stanford, 1964). America's relations with Japan in the mid-1930s receive definitive treatment in Dorothy Borg, *The United States and the Far Eastern Crisis of 1933-1938* (Cambridge, Mass., 1964). See also Samuel Eliot Morison, *The Rising Sun in the Pacific, 1931-April 1942* (*History of United States Naval Operations in World War II,* III, Boston, 1948). For the Spanish civil war there is F. Jay Taylor, *The United States and the Spanish Civil War* (New York, 1956), and Allen Guttman, *The Wound in the Heart: America and the Spanish Civil War* (1962).

Turning to American foreign relations in the years from the *Panay* incident to Pearl Harbor, the leading study is the two-volume work by William L. Langer and S. Everett Gleason, *The Challenge to Isolation, 1937-1940* (New York, 1952). Published by the Council on Foreign Relations, these books rest on exhaustive study of manuscript and printed sources, and it seems unlikely that there will soon appear a better account. In their interpretation, Langer and Gleason have little criticism of American policy. A more compact book covering the same subject—and offering a similar interpretation—is Donald F. Drummond, *The Passing of American Neutrality* (Ann Arbor, 1955). See also Basil Rauch, *Roosevelt: From Munich to Pearl Harbor* (New York, 1950), a somewhat exaggerated defense of Rooseveltian diplomacy, and T.R. Fehrenbach, *F.D.R.'s Undeclared War, 1939 to 1941,* (New York, 1967). For an opposite view, the "revisionist" view that Roosevelt carefully maneuvered the United States to war in 1939-41, there are several books. The best-known is Charles A. Beard, *President Roosevelt and the Coming of the War, 1941* (New Haven, 1948). Other revisionist books are Charles C. Tansill, *Back Door to War,* already mentioned, William Henry Chamberlin, *America's Second Crusade* (Chicago, 1950), Harry Elmer Barnes (ed.), *Perpetual War for Perpetual Peace* (Caldwell, Ida., 1953), and Frederic R. Sanborn, *Design for War: A Study of Secret Power Politics, 1937-1941* (New York, 1951). The revisionist books are argumentative, emphasizing evidence that seems to support the revisionist view, ignoring or "playing down" that which does not. Few scholars take them seriously. A book that offers unusual insight to Roosevelt's thinking on foreign problems in the years just before Pearl Harbor is Robert E. Sherwood, *Roosevelt and Hopkins: An Intimate History* (New York, 1948). For a bibliographical survey see Wayne S. Cole, "American Entry into World War II: A Historiographical Appraisal," *Mississippi Valley Historical Review,* XLIII, March 1957.

There are several books of special importance for America's response to events in Europe in the years before Pearl Harbor. Of particular interest are the brilliant volumes by Winston S. Churchill, *The Second World War,* I, *The Gathering Storm* (Boston, 1948), and II, *Their Finest Hour* (Boston, 1949). See also E. L. Woodward, *British Foreign Policy in the Second World War* (London, 1962). There are four useful studies of relations between the United States and Germany: James V. Compton, *The Swastika and the Eagle: Hitler, the United States, and the Origins of World War II* (Boston, 1967), Saul Friedländer, *Prelude to Downfall: Hitler and the United States, 1939-1941* (New York, 1967), Alton Frye, *Nazi Germany and the American Hemisphere, 1931-1941* (New York, 1967), and Hans L. Trefousse, *Germany and American Neutrality, 1939-1941* (New York, 1951). The United States ambassadors in London and Paris when war broke out in September 1939 were Joseph P. Kennedy and William C. Bullitt. Essays on these two men appear in Gordon A. Craig and Felix Gilbert (eds.), *The Diplomats: 1919-1939* (Princeton, 1953). The standard work on American relations with the Vichy government in France is William L. Langer, *Our Vichy Gamble* (New York, 1947). A critique of Langer is Louis Gottschalk, "Our Vichy Fumble," *Journal of Modern History,* XX, 1948. The best study of the "destroyer deal" of September 1940 is Philip Goodhart, *Fifty Ships that Saved the World: The Foundations of the Anglo-American*

Alliance (Garden City, 1965). An Englishman, Goodhart sees the destroyer-bases transaction as a landmark in the history of the Second World War. There is no satisfactory account of the lend-lease program, but the student will find information in Edward R. Stettinius, Jr., *Lend Lease: Weapon for Victory* (New York, 1944). An excellent analysis of America's decision to extend lend-lease to the Soviet Union is Raymond H. Dawson, *The Decision to Aid Russia, 1941: Foreign Policy and Domestic Politics* (Chapel Hill, N. C., 1959). The best study of American response to the war between Finland and the Soviet Union is Andrew J. Schwartz, *America and the Russo-Finnish War* (Washington, 1960). See also Robert Sobel, *The Origins of Intervention: The United States and the Russo-Finnish War* (New York, 1960). For the naval war in the Atlantic there is Samuel Eliot Morison, *The Battle of the Atlantic, September 1939-May 1943* (*History of United States Naval Operations in World War II,* I, Boston, 1947).

Several books concentrate on American relations with Japan in 1937-41. The standard account is Herbert Feis, *The Road to Pearl Harbor* (New York, 1950). An individual with experience in diplomacy, Feis combined his gifts as a diplomat and historian to produce a brilliant book. His approach is essentially narrative, letting facts speak for themselves, but it is clear that he approves the Far Eastern policies of President Roosevelt. Another good study is David J. Lu, *From the Marco Polo Bridge to Pearl Harbor: Japan's Entry into World War II* (Washington, 1961). For an especially interesting account of events leading to war as viewed from a Japanese perspective, see Robert J. C. Butow, *Tojo and the Coming of the War* (Princeton, 1962). Resting on Japanese sources, this book shows little sympathy for Japanese policy. One of the first books on the origins of war between Japan and America was Walter Millis, *This is Pearl!: The United States and Japan—1941* (New York, 1941). This is an eminently readable book, and its ideas, despite lack of support from manuscript sources, have stood the test of time. For the effect of America's possession of Japan's diplomatic code an excellent book is Ladislas Farago, *The Broken Seal: "Operation Magic" and the Secret Road to Pearl Harbor* (New York, 1967). Was Roosevelt pledged to ask for war in the event of a Japanese attack on British or Dutch territory? See Raymond

A. Esthus, "President Roosevelt's Commitment to Britain to Intervene in the Pacific War," *Mississippi Valley Historical Review,* L, June 1963. Then there are the revisionsts, writers who have considered Pearl Harbor the consequence of a conspiracy in Washington. In addition to revisionist works already mentioned, see George Morgenstern, *Pearl Harbor: The Story of the Secret War* (New York, 1947), and Rear Admiral Robert A. Theobald, *The Final Secret of Pearl Harbor: The Washington Contribution to the Japanese Attack* (New York, 1954). For retorts to revisionist ideas consult Samuel Eliot Morison, "Did Roosevelt Start the War—History Through a Beard," *Atlantic Monthly,* 182, August 1948. A careful analysis of revisionist scholarship is in Robert H. Ferrell, "Pearl Harbor and the Revisionists," *The Historian,* XVII, Spring 1955. For a nonconspiratorial but critical view of Roosevelt's Far Eastern policies see Francis C. Jones, *Japan's New Order in East Asia: Its Rise and Fall, 1937-45* (New York, 1954), and Paul W. Schroeder, *The Axis Alliance and Japanese-American Relations, 1941* (Ithaca, N.Y., 1958). Retorts to the Jones-Schroeder ideas appear in Dexter Perkins, "Was Roosevelt Wrong?," *Virginia Quarterly Review,* XXX, Summer 1954, and Herbert Feis, "War Came at Pearl Harbor: Suspicions Considered," *The Yale Review,* XLV, Spring 1956.

The clearest expression of Japanese strategy—and how Pearl Harbor fitted into it—appears in Samuel Eliot Morison's little masterpiece, *Strategy and Compromise* (Boston, 1958). For the origin and execution of the Pearl Harbor attack see John Deane Potter, *Yamamoto: The Man Who Menaced America* (New York, 1965). A gripping account of the raid appears in Walter Lord, *Day of Infamy* (New York, 1957). First appearing as a special in *Life,* Lord's book rests on interviews of hundreds of Japanese and Americans who witnessed the attack. In some details the Potter and Lord accounts vary, but with patience and logic the reader often can resolve differences. See also Samuel Eliot Morison, *The Rising Sun in the Pacific,* already mentioned, Andrieu D'Albas, *Death of a Navy: Japanese Naval Action in World War II* (New York, 1957), Masanori Ito, *The End of the Imperial Japanese Navy* (New York, 1962), Masatake Okumiya and Jiro Horikoshi, *Zero!* (New York, 1956), Kazuo Sakamaki, *I Attacked Pearl Har-*

bor, (New York, 1949), and U. S. Congress, Joint Committee on the Investigation of the Pearl Harbor Attack, 79th Cong., 1st Sess., Part 13. The question of why Pearl Harbor was "asleep" on December 7, 1941 has tantalized Americans. But not until many years after the attack did a scholar, Roberta Wohlstetter, go to the voluminous records of congressional investigations of the raid and make a careful search for an answer. The result was *Pearl Harbor: Warning and Decision* (Stanford, 1962). The author presents an impressive case for the idea that weaknesses in America's system of gathering and evaluating intelligence data were largely responsible for surprise at Pearl Harbor. A similar view appears in Samuel Eliot Morison's *Two-Ocean War* (Boston, 1963), a condensation of his multivolume naval history. Another interesting book is A. A. Hoehling, *The Week Before Pearl Harbor* (New York, 1963). Hoehling finds "apathy" in the government in Washington to blame for the Pearl Harbor disaster. For a defense of the commanders at Pearl Harbor see Husband E. Kimmel, *Admiral Kimmel's Story* (Chicago, 1955). The reader wishing to go to source materials on Pearl Harbor might consult one of the two collections of excerpts from testimony given in congressional hearings: Hans L. Trefousse (ed.), *What Happened at Pearl Harbor* (New York, 1958), and Paul S. Burtness and Warren U. Ober (eds.), *The Puzzle of Pearl Harbor* (Evanston, Ill., 1962).

INDEX